THE GIRL WITH RED HAIR

THE GIRL WITH RED HAIR

MUSINGS ON A THEME

Edited by

Thomas E. Kennedy and Walter Cummins

SERVING HOUSE BOOKS

The Girl with Red Hair

The two poems by Laura McCullough originally appeared in the on-line magazine *Oranges and Sardines*.

ISBN: 978-0-9826921-6-5

Cover photo by Lotte Mia Wewer

Serving House Books logo by Barry Lereng Wilmont

Published by Serving House Books
Copenhagen and Florham Park, NJ

www.servinghousebooks.com

First Serving House Books Edition 2011

CONTENTS

7   Preface

9   The Short Time of Smiling, *Lance Olsen*

14   Marie, Beside the River, *H.L. Hix*

16   Unheard Melodies, *Tom Dunn*

21   L'Auteur des Choses, *Thomas E. Kennedy*

28   Guide to the Outer Islands, *Robert Stewart*

30   His Mother's Child, *Walter Cummins*

35   The Lilies of Wolf Creek, *Susan Tekulve*

46   Ruby-in-a-Bottle, *Renée Ashley*

47   My Red Desdemona, *David R. Poe*

56   Laughter in the Dark, *Niels Hav*

57   Other People's Problems, *Ladette Randolph*

60   Danger, *Pamela Painter*

64   A Photo of My Mother, 1972, *Steve Kowit*

66   Fluent, *Alexandra Marshall*

71   Gwen, Betsy and Anne Marie Jensen, *Dorthe Nors*

81   Nine Lives of the Cougar, *Duff Brenna*

93   What We Want, *Laura McCullough*

95   Beauty Salon Love, *Laura McCullough*

97   Collector, *Line-Maria Lång*

100 Cayenne Pepper, *Steve Heller*

119 About the Editors

120 About the Authors and Translators

PREFACE

People with red hair-—estimated as two percent of the human population—have been feared, disdained, admired, and associated with supernatural attributes.   For their flame-like color, they have been branded with a fiery hot temper and passionate nature. Sylvia Plath evokes a powerful threat in the female: "Out of the ash / I rise with my red hair / And eat men like air."   This menace is echoed in a Gaelic Storm lyric: "Green eyes, red hair long legs / Devil inside her / Green eyes, red hair, long legs / Devil inside her." Mark Twain saw the rest of us descended from apes but redheads from cats. How can we resist them?

Inspired by poems, lyrics, and legends, but most immediately, the photograph on the cover of this book, we invited nineteen established authors to write a story, poem, or essay that took the photograph as its point of departure. We hope that our readers will be compelled and entertained by the redheads who comprise this anthology.

Here, then, is to the one or two out of a hundred redheads or gingers or copper-tops or carrot-heads in our world—as well as to the redheads among our authors, a few of whom are in fact gingers and others with redheads in their immediate families.

A special thanks to Line-Maria Lång whose photo graces our cover and served as our muse.

–Thomas E. Kennedy and Walter Cummins
Copenhagen and Florham Park, NJ

THE SHORT TIME OF SMILING

Lance Olsen

One drizzly spring morning, the first bobbed to the surface of the graygreen river rilling through town. An old woman walking her terrier dropped her rhinestone leash and began screaming, and a moment later a flurry of gesticulating bystanders had gathered to watch the blue-sweatered arm point at the sky and disappear beneath the water, point at the sky and disappear, become a brief white agitation, and then become nothing at all.

Volunteers searched for the body downstream for three days before giving up. On the way back to town at twilight, they saw the second. Another sweatered arm (gold this time, not blue) pointing at the sky and disappearing, except much nearer the riverbank.

Several men still boyish enough to be dedicated to the idea of gallantry shed their coats and shirts and shoes and tumbled into the rush.

They returned with a beautiful human-sized doll. A brightly flowered dress clung to her pale rubber skin. Her right arm held the remains of a real cigarette, saturated and half-smoked. Her left wasn't pointing at the sky at all, they came to realize, but rather touching her long astonishing hair the color of hope and sadness. Some argued her expression was the embodiment of peacefulness, others of dispassion. Some contended it was simply what faces of the dead did, relieved as they were finally to be shut of the world, the noisy living, the spiky sea urchin in a clutched palm called life.

In the town square stood the guildhall. They laid the doll out on the heavy oak table in the middle of the otherwise barren main room to examine her for identifying marks. Two men in the group secretly prayed she was an automaton, one a blind river nymph. Four worried she wasn't a doll, but the shadow of an angel or manifestation of a cat's soul. After much inspecting, they concluded there were no panels to open, no mechanical insides to discover, no organs to detect, no otherworldly traces—just the perfect simulation of a young woman's body.

Everyone could smell (but refused to acknowledge) the distractingly gratifying fragrance of patchouli, shaded with a faint whiff of plastic and dirty water, emanating from the doll.

Her lips, several of the men thought to themselves, sneaking glances at each another. Her lips.

Next morning the doll's half-smoked cigarette was gone. Someone had stolen it. That afternoon the third doll appeared on the grassy slope leading down to the river. A couple pushing a stroller nearby swore the spot had been empty when they approached it. They said they had closed their eyes simultaneously to feel the sunshine upon their faces, as recently married couples sometimes do, and when they opened them again the spot wasn't empty anymore. It was hectic with a doll several centimeters shorter than the other that weighed slightly less and flaunted hair somewhere between the color of heart blizzards and the hour of the wolf.

The townspeople carried her to the guildhall to keep the other one company on the heavy oak table, assuring themselves as they went that the situation was a simple anomaly, a rarity, an existential one-off. Perhaps, they told each other, somewhere up the river lived a doddering doll maker. Perhaps there had been an accident. Perhaps someone had found this one in the water, plucked her out, carried her up onto the grassy slope, and walked away. Perhaps it was as simple as that, they said, knowing a lie when they heard one.

The following Sunday no one could help noticing the pews were less full than usual. The following Monday many employees failed to turn up for work. Managers at the brewery and the inn on the outskirts of town became angry. Several shops were forced to close early, while several cafés never opened.

What happened the next day made that one feel exactly like the birth of any other week. What happened the next day was that beautiful human-sized dolls began winking into existence everywhere—on park benches and fountain steps, trams and library carrels, hospital gurneys and bar booths. Some sat properly, some with egregiously splayed legs. Some reclined like queens two hours before beheadings, and some were found propped upright against stone walls like so many wooden posts. Each was touching her breathtaking hair, each smoking the cigarette that never diminished, and, while some were tall and some squat and some lean and some plump, all possessed those lips that dogged every man and many women deep into their dreams.

It wasn't long before crisply dressed businessmen, heads high and backs straight, appeared carrying them under their arms like briefcases. Teachers dragged them in their wakes like sacks of wheat. Laborers showed up at eateries with them slung onto their backs like rucksacks or angry fathers, asking for tables for two.

Meanwhile women befriended them, could be seen sitting across from them at the cement chess boards sprinkled throughout town, leaning forward, whispering, sharing confidences they would never have shared with another human being.

Sometimes women brought them back to their beds when their men were away.

Sometimes women invited their husbands or boyfriends to join them when they returned home.

It became common to find funerals populated by more dolls than people, because everyone knew it was always more important to have a bigger audience of replacement mourners at your obsequy than a collection of real friends while you were alive.

These days came to be known as The Short Time of Smiling. During this season, single people found partners. Professors found students. Proselytizers found apostles. Doctors found patients. And politicians found congregations who believed the outrageous stories they had to tell.

As weeks turned into months, months into years, new dolls stopped materializing. One day the townspeople woke to the understanding there hadn't been a new one in their lives for nearly a decade. And the ones already there had commenced showing their age, as beautiful human-sized dolls will. Their clothes had gradually dated, worn out, and had been replaced with sweaters and dresses that were inexplicably less appealing than the originals. Their bodies had become blemished by scuffmarks, scurf, smeared lipstick stains, rips, cuts, punctures, and indelible ink tattoos. Their fingers had eroded like pencil erasers. In many cases their knuckles had snapped, their legs dropped off, their eyes popped out unexpectedly.

The days that had come to be known as The Short Time of Smiling drifted into the days that came to be known as The Long Wrappings of Regret.

Money ran low, and so people returned to work.

Happiness ran low, and so people returned to themselves.

And about that time a bone composer happened to pass through town. Like most bone composers, he was half the height of normal people, half as good-looking, and half as intelligent. Sometimes when someone was speaking to him he would unthinkingly allow his tongue to fall out of his mouth and loll on his chin like a pet. Sometimes he smelled of mildew.

Despite these shortcomings, the manager of the inn was only too happy to overcharge the artist for his room and board while telling him The History of the Dolls. In turn, the bone composer offered his services. He believed, he said, he might be able to help with the current circumstances, at least a little. The manager led him directly over to the guildhall where the city council happened to be meeting.

The very next day the bone composer set to work. For the first week, he labored alone, collecting abandoned dolls and doll parts and carrying them down to the grassy slope by the river to the exact spot where the doll had winked into existence all that time ago. When he commenced arranging those dolls and doll parts into new formations, bystanders began to gather. When he started to add the new formations to further new formations, the town librarian stepped out of the crowd to help him. The trash collector soon followed, then that old woman who had been walking her terrier.

And before long the whole town was busily assisting the bone composer erect an assemblage larger than anything anyone had ever seen: a doll twice the height of the church spire made out of beat-up, smudged, and sometimes charred human-sized doll torsos, hands, legs, feet, and arms, some clothed, some naked, some hairless, some hooded, and not one in its rightful place.

Everybody expected something miraculous to occur in the end, but it didn't. When the bone composer and townspeople had finally finished their undertaking, nothing much had changed. No one was particularly happier or sadder than before. The divorce rate remained constant. No one shed a fear or a disease. No one grew younger. No one grew wiser. And the people in nearby towns? They couldn't have cared less about the nativity of the monster doll.

Still, at about three o'clock on a frisky autumn afternoon a short time later, the bone composer was tilling his field behind the small hut on the outskirts of town he had been paid by the council for his dubious efforts. He stopped and stood up straight for a moment to remove his hat and wipe his brow, and that's when he noticed, briefly, that his back didn't ache. His teeth were still by and large in his mouth, if undeniably the worse for wear. A large hare hunched in the corner of his vision. Behind him, unnoticed, someone's boy fell out of the sky. There was nothing more the bone composer was interested in possessing. There was no one he especially envied, no one he knew of who especially envied him. It didn't hurt particularly much to know he was aging just like everybody else, or that he had only a small handful of people he could call friends, or that he had wanted to end up doing that but ended up doing this.

And so he almost smiled, or at least almost thought about it for a heartbeat or two, and then he leaned back into his plow and pushed ahead.

MARIE, BESIDE THE RIVER
H. L. Hix

Her name was Marie. She had red hair.
This was long ago. Now nothing's the same.
          Her name was Marie. When they blew toward her,
leaves glided, graceful as birds. And why not?
She had red hair that registered
how far we all are on our way to winter.
Teenage lovers gathered there
as if it were a park where they
could neck while others played guitar
or watched their dogs chase squirrels.
          This was long ago. The part of me
she restored lived its moth-length life.
Happy people punted past,
one with sleeves rolled up to row,
the other to trail one arm the way
a drowsy willow trails its branches.
          She had red hair, she had long fingers.
She winced with each drag, but still I envied
her cigarettes those fingers, those lips.
She winced again when she exhaled.
She squinted in the river-bent light.
          Now nothing's the same. Women bend down,
adjust the children in their strollers.
Laughter from couples at one with the current

competes with the clapping of pigeons scattering
from a man bracing his cane to stand.
To see her now, I have to squint.

Her name was Marie. She had red freckles.
Her hair when she lay back in grass
was thick enough to cover clover.
Retrievers, giddy in the river,
appeared as heads with wakes like wings.

This, all of this, was long ago:
the park, the river, the city, Marie,
her hair spread out across the grass,
the first leaves, the last clover.
The unsteady man leaving behind
a bench and bread crumbs and regathered birds.
Her cigarette held up to catch songs:
couples laughing through willow limbs,
dogs shaking off water, one
uncertain guitar, mothers humming
to soothe their children back to sleep.

This one red hair was hers, is her.
Now nothing's Marie. Her name is Long Ago.

UNHEARD MELODIES

Tom Dunne

He first saw her in Versailles. She lay on the bank of the lake, her red hair fanned out around her in the green grass, eyes closed, berry-colored lips in sweet repose, complexion white as ivory. She wore a full, flowered dress and open yellow sweater, her left hand resting in her hair, elbow crooked above her. At first he thought she was asleep. But then he noticed she was holding a cigarette in her other hand, poised above her breast as though she had been about to move it to her lips but dropped off to sleep halfway. It was a home-rolled cigarette. Maybe, he thought, she was afloat in a reefer dream, hearing a melody that was beyond hearing.

He stepped closer. It occurred to him that she was the most beautiful woman he had ever seen. Not that she was objectively so beautiful, although she was that, but that she radiated beauty. She looked like a cover illustration for a collection of poems by Keats.

Because her eyes were closed, he felt free to look directly at her, filled his gaze with her over and over. The thought struck him, ridiculous as it seemed, that he had fallen in love with a stranger, that the image of her would haunt him as long as he lived. He realized, of course, how irrational and unlikely this was, how ridiculous, and the realization made him look away, focus on the surface of the lake that mirrored the pale blue sky. A man paddled a rowboat in the center. A cumulus of green trees rose on the opposite bank. She was very young, too, he thought, perhaps half his fifty years.

He looked at her again and fell in love once again, more deeply now. It was not lust he felt. It felt like a higher passion she inspired in him. At that moment she opened her eyes. His instinct was to avert his gaze, but two things held him: first, the startling, even shocking, even perhaps frightening color of her eyes—a milky blue almost devoid of color yet at the same time brilliant; second, the fact that she smiled with welcome at him.

A welcoming smile from a woman, he had concluded in his years, can be surrender or invitation; this smile was neither and both and something quite other as well. What could he do but return it and say, "Hello," and hope that she might become part of his life and he of hers.

Holding his gaze in hers, she moved the reefer to her lips and drew deeply, then held it out to him. He stooped to receive it, toked, then sat beside her on the grass. She rose up on her elbows, and he remembered an earlier loss and desired to be with her so strongly that all thoughts of his life back in Albany vanished in that desire. Perhaps he thought this would be or could be a separate part of his life, an episode on a journey, that it would not touch his family, that he could live this piece of his fate only for the few days that remained to him in Paris, then could complete his business here and return, unchanged yet somehow fulfilled—finally would have tasted that fullness of something he had only before glimpsed, would have participated somehow in her beauty. A secret that he would lock inside and take out only when he was alone to be renewed by it.

Whatever it was in the cigarette emboldened him. He said, "I feel I have to tell you something. To ask you something."

She tilted her head, a smile fluttering on her lips.

He thought that he must tell it indirectly, that to go directly into it might jeopardize this sense of vision, of imminent discovery. So he said, "Once, some time ago, I was in a very distant, very exotic place. I saw a woman in a flowing robe walking across a grassy field. She was carrying a staff and had long flowing hair—hair the color of yours—and she had an aura. She was charismatic. Something at once spiritual and sensual. I felt very strongly that I should call out to her, should talk to her."

The girl with red hair passed the joint again, and he drew on it, handed it back. "But I couldn't think of anything to say," he went on. "So she kept walking, and I watched her get farther and farther away. And then she was gone, and I was left only with a profound sense of loss."

She watched her fingers tamping out the stub of reefer in the grass, and she seemed to be deciding something, perhaps what she would say. Finally she looked up, her milky-blue eyes level on his. "The way you described that woman," she said. "I so understand that. I so understand."

He looked into her eyes, her astonishing eyes. "Come back to Paris with me," he said. "Let's have dinner together."

§

She seemed dreamy on the RER train back to Paris, and he sat in a seat over from her but leaning forward and holding her hand in both of his. Her palm was cool and dry and very soft and the touch of her pale white fingers on the ruddy backs of his hands was intricately delicate; he thought he had never felt such an intricate touch before. She smiled so dreamily, her eyelids half-lowered, as though she were halfway in a dream, hearing that melody only she could hear within the quiet hum of the train's rubber wheels. They had exchanged few words, as though words might break the spell of their meeting. She was from Stockholm, was living in a borrowed apartment in the fourth, was alone in Paris.

He was staying on rue Git-le-Coeur in the sixth on the other side of the Seine from her, and he had suggested that they get off at Saint-Michel and have dinner at Le Petit Zinc on rue Saint-Benoit where they had a splendid variety of *huitres* and where he thought her red hair would be perfect among the *Belle Époque* style.

They switched to the Metro at Issy and had to stand amidst the jostling crowd, but squeezed in around the pole, and he held her hand and thought they had not even told their names yet. He was trying not to plan ahead, to let things happen as they must. He had four days left and only a few hours of business to complete—the day after tomorrow—and his brain was awash with excitement. He wanted to get her to the restaurant—no, first an *aperitif* at the Café Flor—champagne—or rather outside at Les Deux Magots—it was warm enough to sit outside—yes, right across from St-Germain-des-Prés, an ancient church where the Vikings had been—he would tell her that as they sipped champagne—he would show her things that he had learned in his life, in all his years.

At Invalides, a very large man with a very large piece of baggage forced himself between them. It seemed comic—his great girth, his sweaty face, his black hair plastered to his forehead, the huge piece of baggage hugged to him like an unwieldy lover. He and the girl met each other's eyes and their lips lumped with suppressed laughter, and the man, with a great heave, repositioned his bag, breaking the grip of their hands. He glanced up at the station map above the doors and tried to look around the man's large head and mouth the words, *Next stop—Saint-Michel.* Bodies crowded in around him, and he could not see her face—only one eye and the corner of her mouth.

"Next stop," he said aloud. "Saint-Michel."

The train rolled to a stop, and the doors slid open. "Come on," he called to her. "Hurry, it's now!" And moved with the flow of bodies onto the platform. He could not turn for a moment, managed to slip through two blocky women each with two bulging net bags just in time to see the doors close and her red flowing hair behind the big sweaty-faced man as the train pulled out of the station.

§

At the seafood bar beyond the security check in Charles de Gaulle, he ordered six huitres and a split of champagne, spooned relish on the one oyster, forked it into his mouth, then swallowed the fluid in the shell and chased it with champagne. He held the shell for a moment, gazing loiteringly into its pale interior before dropping it into the bed of shaved ice. There were nearly two hours to take-off, and he waited a bit before spooning relish on the next oyster, but soon anyway he was down to his last and only half a flute of champagne remained.

§

He had waited at Saint-Michel, thinking that what people did when separated on the Metro was to stay on the platform and let the one left in the train come back. The one in the train knew where the one on the platform was. Wasn't that how it went? He remembered a nightmare he'd had as a child of being separated on the frightening Manhattan subway from his mother. He'd told her about the dream, and she said that if that ever happened, if he was on the platform, he should stay put; if he was in the train, he should get off at the next stop and stay put. So he waited an hour on Saint-Michel, then took the metro to the next stop, Saint-Michel Notre-Dame, and waited there for another hour.

Most of the remainder of his free time he spent wandering the fourth. Then he got to wondering whether he had actually mentioned either Café Flor, Les Deux Magots or Le Petit Zinc to her. So he sat visibly, by turn, at a street table in each of the three places for a couple of hours.

Finally, then, on his last morning in the city, having given up hope, as he walked along the Quai Saint-Michel, passing Shakespeare And Company, he spied a red-haired woman standing by the counter, her back to the window, paying for a book, chatting with the young man at the register. Feeling like Omar Sharif on a bus in Moscow spying Julie Christie on the street from behind, he hurried in, daring not to hope, and touched her shoulder.

The young woman turned, still smiling from something the young man behind the counter had said to her. "Hey!" she said. "How are you?"

He looked at her. "I'm leaving for the airport in an hour."

"Oh," she said. "Sad."

§

Now, in the airport, he ate the last oyster and looked into the empty shell and saw himself as a creature driven and derided by vanity, and his eyes burned with anguish and anger.

L'AUTEUR DES CHOSES

Thomas E. Kennedy

M y name is Tom Dunne. I am an author. I am, in fact, the author of things. I am creating the world of this story into which you, hopefully, are being drawn.

But ordinarily this would be a lonely story. It would make you sad. Or at least it would make me sad. All my stories do. But this story is not going to make me sad. Because in this story I have decided I am going to meet a beautiful woman. I will create her just for myself, and she will be perfect, and we will not make each other sad. We will make each other happy.

She will be a redhead. A beautiful redhead, sleeping by a lake in late afternoon sunlight. There she is right now. Do you see her? She is lying in the grass on the bank of a lake—or perhaps a river. Yes, a river. The Seine. This story takes place in Paris. In the heat of August when most Parisians are away. The girl's brilliant red hair is fanned out in the deep-green grass. Her eyes are closed, and the hand of one arm, crooked at the elbow, rests languidly in her thick hair. The other hand hovers over her breast, holding a joint in her soft, ivory-white fingers. Yes. A beautiful red head with beautiful pale red lips and skin the white of an ivory sculpture in the grass by the river, dreamy on pot. She could be the cover illustration for an anthology of British Romantic poetry. And she is mine. She is my creation.

I step closer to her and softly say, "Open your eyes. Tell me your name." I like to give my characters a little bit of free will—not much, just a little. It would be boring otherwise.

Her eyelids flutter open to reveal a surprise. I did not know what startlingly luminous pale blue eyes she would have. She stares at me, looking startled, as if surprised to find herself here, in this story.

"What is your name?" I ask again.

"I am Lorelei," she says. She has an accent I cannot quite place. Nordic perhaps. She looks at the reefer between her fingers as though uncertain what it is. Then she looks at me again with those luminous eyes.

"Who are you?" she asks.

"Dunne is the name. Tom Dunne. The author." I wonder if she will understand that when I say "the" author I mean the author of this story. As I try to decide what I wish to make happen next, there comes a splashing from the river, and another woman with red hair crawls up onto the grassy bank like a molting butterfly, water sliding from her close-cropped curly red locks, rolling down her shoulders and chest. She rises. She is wearing an aquamarine two-piece swim suit and her skin is tanned and alluring.

"Who are you?!" I ask, more an exclamation than a question. I didn't create her. What is she doing in my story? She may have come from my pen, but not from my imagination—in any event, she was not a conscious act of my imagination, and I wonder if my imagination has its own volition, if it hovers in shadowy corners into which I cannot see and subverts my purposes. I recall a debate between Forster and Nabokov in which someone asked Forster if his characters sometimes seemed to have a will of their own, and he answered that indeed they did, whereupon Nabokov said that he could well understand if the passengers mutinied on that dreary voyage to India but that his characters were galley slaves. Do my characters have free will? Do I? *[Questions for study: Can a character in a fiction have 'free will'?]*

The sun is in the western sky, sliding toward the horizon, and I notice suddenly how hot and muggy it has become. I did not ask this other red-head to rise from the water of the river. Nonetheless a quick glance at her and into her eyes—the same luminous blue!—assures me, as though it were the will of another, that I want her here.

"What is your name?" I ask.

"You can call me Dot, honey," she says in that same strange accent as Lorelei's. She looks me up and down and says, "And what should I call you other than honey, honey?"

Lorelei says, "He's Tom." She says it in a way that is almost a question – as though I were the intruder.

"Tom?" says Dot. "Well how are your caramels, honey?"

Lorelei claps her soft white hand over her lips and giggles.

"My caramels?" I ask, confused. Am I being goaded by my own creations. Made an object of ridicule.

Dot smiles owlishly. "Haven't you ever heard of Tom's caramels?"

"I'm Tom Dunne," I say and straighten my shoulders. "The author," I add with dignity.

"Author of the caramels," says Dot, and I feel the situation slipping from my grasp. In a bid for control, I ask, "Where are you girls from?" Yet feel that I should know the answer to that already. This is my story. And it is set in Paris, I remind myself. These girls, with their strange northern accent, could only be foreigners. Sweden, I think—perhaps I will make them be from Sweden. Like Anita Ekberg in Fellini's *Dolce Vita*, dancing in that Roman fountain, perhaps I will create a fountain for them to dance in!

"We're from Jutland," says Lorelei.

For a moment I can't remember where Jutland is. "Well you're in Paris now," I insist, still thinking with one part of my mind what kind of fountain I would like to create for them to dance in.

"Well, honey, haven't you ever heard of a Jutlandish girl with a bone in her nose?"

"With a...? Say, are you getting risqué?" I demand. "This is not that kind of story. This is a romantic story" So the kitty is out of the bag. This is a story. That should put them in place. They are mere characters! I, *au contraire*, am the author.

"You *think* it's not that kind of story, honey. Once you let Jutlandish girls in the door, it could turn into any kind of story."

"You're kind of fresh," I say—but at the same time recognize that, despite myself, I am drawn to her *[Question for study: Why does Tom Dunne here say "despite myself"? What is this a possible example of?]*

"You bet I'm fresh, honey!"

Lorelei at that moment slides the joint between her sweet, berry-red lips and takes a deep toke on it, as though suddenly discovering that after all she knows exactly what it is there for. She holds the smoke deep in her lungs, then coughs some of it out and begins to pass it to Dot, but draws back, saying, "Dry your fingers first, Dot." She says this in a familiar, even intimate manner as though they know each other already, even intimately.

Dot does as she is asked, then takes a perfunctory hit before passing it to me, but withholds it teasingly. "Don't Bogart that thang, honey!"

"He's Tom," Lorelei says again for some reason—as though imparting some other subliminal information, and as I take a hit they look knowingly at one another, then go into a dance routine, singing to the tune of "Juan Tanamera":

"Tom's caramel-els! Oh yes it's Tom's carmel-els! Tom's car-a-mel-els! Oh yes it's Tom's caramel-els!"

They kick their long shapely legs in unison, right leg left, left leg right, snapping their fingers and staring at me with their four luminous eyes.

Abruptly, then, they stop and Dot, with an amused smile, says, "You thought you could write yourself right into a big juicy ménage a trois, didn't you, honey?"

"No," I say. "No! That is not what I meant at all. I am not like that. I am not at all like that. I have respect for my characters. 'Almost astonishing respect and tenderness for his characters,' one of the reviewers said, in fact. And by the way, Dot: I didn't even write *you*!"

"Well, excuse me for breathing, honey!"

"Don't misunderstand," I say. "You're welcome in the story. I like you."

"But you're threatened, honey, is that it? Because you didn't know that we are authors as well. Any one of us could be 'the' author."

"*What*?!" I demand. "What do you mean by that? I am the author!"

Dot looks into my eyes with a pity that is almost tender and, affecting a British accent, says, "Honey, you are the caretaker. You have always been the caretaker."

[Questions for study: Is it possible that 'Tom Dunne' is not the author? If so, name one other possibility who the author might be? And what is 'Dot'

24

referring to when she says that 'Tom Dunne' is 'the caretaker'?]

At that moment there is a splashing from the river and another woman emerges. She is shaved bald but has two lush clumps of copper red hair beneath her shapely arms. She is wearing a vest and jeans which are plastered wet to her, and she appears astonished to find herself in this company.

"Who the hell are you?" I demand, but Dot laughs. "Ha! That's the bitch you were so taken by at the Pathetic Bureau on the north side last winter. It was her debut reading. You couldn't stop thinking about her."

I gasp. "How did you know about her?!"

"Honey, I have access."

Lorelei and Dot begin to teach the bald girl their dance routine, and soon the three of them are kicking in unison and snapping their fingers, singing, "Tom's caramel-els!" to the tune of "Juan Tanamera" and staring at me with their six eyes—which are all equally luminously blue.

They are dancing toward me as I back away, gasping, "This is not the story I set out to write!"

"Oh, honey," says Dot with a mild smirk, rotating her fists beneath her elbows and shaking her breasts as she continues to dance, and the two others shake their breasts in synchrony—six breasts shaking in my face, but not in the way I would have written it.

"This is your story, honey—the story of your life, honey! You Dunne done it!"

"But this was meant to be a happy story!" I scream.

"Don't you think *we're* happy, honey? We're *very* happy. You just didn't realize that we are all authors, too. All of us. Maybe you created us that way. Or maybe we created *you*. To tease and torment. Or maybe to liberate."

"To liberate from what?" I ask, feeling a sense of creeping horror.

But she only smiles and, glancing knowingly at Lorelei and the bald woman with copper-red armpit hair, says, "Anyone's guess who 'the' author is here, isn't that right, honey?"

I back farther away as they continue to advance, kicking in unison, right leg left, left leg right, snapping the fingers of their six hands, rotating their six fists under their six elbows, their six blue eyes glowing at me, their six breasts quivering. With a glint in her luminous eye, Dot says, "It is a hungry dance we do on monsieur's sword," and seized by inexplicable terror—though I know it is unwise to do so—I turn my back and run. *Never turn your back on the breasts!*

Up the stone steps to the Pompidou Quai, across the Pont Louis Philippe and Pont St. Louis to the Ile de la Cité, through the shadow of Notre Dame whose gargoyles are now all, unaccountably, stiff pricks—I hear Dot calling out behind me, "Are we keeping you up, honey?", followed by a cackling from many female throats. My leather heels sound against the cobblestones. I am panting. I feel a stitch in my side, and my face is slick with sweat in the muggy heat, my shirt plastered to my back and chest.

I cross to the left bank, daring not to look back for I can hear the tramp of their running feet not far behind, and there are certainly more than six tramping feet behind me now. I duck down Rue St. Julien and flatten myself in a narrow alley, and their pounding feet stampede past, and I was right, there are many more of them now, an army of red-headed women authors, taking over the left bank, taking over the story, taking over. What havoc are they seeking to wreak?

As the last of them trample past, I slip out of the alley and move with stealth in the shadows close to the wall, back toward the Seine. They are chanting. I can hear them in the distance:

"Dunne done it! Let's do Dunne! Dunne done it! Let's do Dunne!"

The city is bathed in shadow, the shadow of a de Chirico, of a Hopper black-and-white night shadow woodprint. I can see the red-headed women in the distance, running to and fro in the dark street, casting long frantic primitive shadows . Then the chant begins to move closer again.

"Dunne done it! Let's do Dunne!" A single voice—I think it is the bald woman—calls out, "Let's *undo* Dunne!" followed by a cacophony of cackles.

Panting, sweating, I slip into the next alley just in time to see a man emerging from the shadows. I gasp! It is Robert Coover. He staggers out, muttering, "Who fahrd that shot? Mart fahrd it!" Behind him comes William S. Burroughs, natty in a Burberry buckled around his narrow waist, saying with dry-throated sarcasm, "I never met a Dane who was not bone dull." After him comes Nabokov, eyes brimming with disdain: "Cackling red-headed women taking liberties with the narrative! You, sir, are a *poor* author!"

As if inspired – perhaps by the unexpected appearance of this trio of innovative writers, I realize that this is the Red-Headed Women's Liberation Army of Authors, and as their thundering footsteps move closer, suddenly I understand everything – except who they are, and why they are after me, and what is going to happen. I stand sweating in the alley. It is August, and the heat is enough to drive a man mad.

And the story is not over yet.

[Question for study: What does 'Tom Dunne' suddenly understand in the alley?]

GUIDE TO THE OUTER ISLANDS

Robert Stewart

Laying myself down in the passing lane
of North Lindbergh years back, by then
Sunday morning, leaving the beer joint so far
past midnight, Bob, my absolute sidekick,
had time to drag my body back to the gravel lot,
big as I was compared to him, and take my keys.
This was after the redhead drove off,
leaving a scrap of paper with a phone number
but driving off, nonetheless; Bud neon
flickered in the window and popped
to black. *You always go for the redheads*,
Bob said, as if he knew, as should I, desire
for red hair leads nowhere. The Red Queen,
herself, said it takes all the running you can do
to stay in one place. In mid Lindbergh,
facing up and spread eagle, one could fly
to the outer islands, then, their houses
roofed with grass, to hunt and eat whales
and wind-dried fish from the angry sea.
The dark-haired one really liked you,
Bob would say, friend and counselor,
knowing redheads were impossible to me

in a neighborhood of dark, Sicilian girls;
but among the tables, smoke, and ashes,
arms swinging as the night turned late,
there seemed to appear some signal fire,
a hyacinthine flower of the Faeroes or Finland—
a boreal copper sky swirling among bands
of light in the juke, filling the jar on the bar
with the pale-blue eggs of a gannet, perhaps
like the blouse of Mary. Forgive me, you girls
and cousins of Italy; so skinny were you
in your short, black, Gina Lollobrigida hair,
I didn't know your beauty or how you loved me.
I wanted to turn toward the sky, myself;
and Bob would say to me, *Hair that red
isn't even real*, nor, I knew, was the spark
ignited at their phony ends, good friend
and only purveyor of truth. *So what?*
he'd say. So she drove off in the top-down
Karmann Ghia, the little bottle rocket
of her hair on North Lindbergh going dark
and refiring at each light standard, as far,
at least, as the Shell at Charbonier.

HIS MOTHER'S CHILD

Walter Cummins

When he rounded the corner of his house on the river and saw Claudine lying on the grass, Vaughn's first instinct was to shout, "Put that thing out!" But he knew she would just suck hard and hold it in her mouth, lips pursed, no smoke emerging. Then she would swallow as if to spite him. He imagined the slight tightening of her throat muscles. In fact, he said nothing and she did not move, the joint held in two fingers of a hand that rested on her breast, her eyes closed, fingers of the other hand reaching back into the flaming red hair spread out behind her. An explosion of red on the dark green of the grass.

From where he stood Vaughn couldn't see the baby though he knew it lay beside her in a yellow bunting that matched her sweater, the soft curls of his hair already as red as hers. The boy was all Claudine, without hints of Vaughn's son, James, in his face nor of him or Almeda, as if the child had no father, no paternal lineage.

The girl—young woman—kept the child with her constantly, rarely let anyone else hold him and hovered whenever Almeda pleaded for the opportunity, hands held out like claws, ready to snatch him back. "That's enough," she would say. Vaughn had never seen her pass the boy to James, even when he offered to help, to relieve her. "Not now," she always told him. "I'm not ready."

Yet they had given her a home, made no objection when Vaughn and James and Almeda collected her at the hospital the morning after she had given birth. "Where will you go?" Almeda had asked her before the delivery, when the girl lay on a gurney, a white sheet covering the mound of her middle. "I have no idea," she had answered, very calmly as if it were not a problem.

Out in the waiting room Vaughn had shaken his head when Almeda told him they had to bring her to their home. "I don't think that's such a good idea." And he had turned to James for an affirmation, but James sat stunned, staring out at a blank green wall, as if he were witnessing an accident. "It's James' baby," Almeda had said. "Our grandchild."

Vaughn never called the girl anything to her face, Red when he spoke about her to Almeda and James, even though Almeda each time told him, "Her name is Claudine." When they were alone, he would ask Almeda, "How long?" And Almeda gave a silent shrug that reminded him of a whimper.

He wished Claudine would stay in her room, what for years had been the guest room, next to theirs at the other end of the hallway from James'. But most of the time she spent with them in the kitchen or living room, lurking he called it, rarely speaking, her only sounds the whispers to the baby she cradled in her arms. The baby was just as quiet, except for the occasional times it screamed half the night, Vaughn furious, wrapping a pillow around his head.

A jon boat emerged from behind a cluster of trees at a bend in the river, silently propelled by an electric motor, sun glinting off the aluminum hull. Two fishermen sat with rods across their knees on their way to another place, where the fish were. Vaughn could hear the murmur of their voices but not make out any words. Claudine did not open her eyes, though he was sure she wasn't sleeping.

In frustration he moved toward her, kicking his sandals at the grass, trying to make noise. He squatted beside her, then—when his knees ached—sat with his legs folded in front of him. The marijuana odor drifted toward his face, and he turned away. Inside the house with the family she smoked only cigarettes, saved the joints for the seclusion of her room. It didn't matter. The pungency filled the air.

Almeda never referred to it, though once, in her reticent way, she had asked when the living room was thick with cigarette smoke, "Do you think that's good for the baby?" And Claudine had responded with half a laugh.

"Oh, it's all right." Vaughn had tried to speak to James about it–"Can't you get her to stop?"–and it was as if he had slapped his son's face. At last James said, "I can't get her to do anything."

Here on the grass only a few feet away, Vaughn wondered what would happen if he reached out and snatched the joint from her fingers, ground it into the dirt. But all he did was say, "If you really loved that baby, you wouldn't do that."

She swept her free hand through her red hair, spread it fuller on the grass behind her, eyes still closed. Vaughn watched her closely, felt his own fingers moving in tandem with hers. Then, as he knew she would, she drew deeply on the joint, rolled the smoke in her mouth, and then released it through her curved tongue.

"It makes me feel good."

"And your child's health?"

"He's much better off with a mother who's happy."

"Can't you be happy just being a mother?"

"This makes me even happier. Much happier."

"So your happiness matters more than anything else."

Her eyes still closed, she pointed the glowing tip of the joint at him, punctuating her words with up and down gestures. "No, his does. We all show our love in different ways."

As if in response, the baby let out an open-mouthed sound, not a cry, more like an exclamation of surprise at finding himself alive in the world. His eyes opened wide and, for a few seconds, his arms and legs thrashed in the yellow bunting. Claudine handed Vaughn the joint without asking if he would take it. Her hands free, she lifted the boy high over her head and smiled at his wiggling. She brought him down to lie on her chest, closing an arm around his back and touching her lips to the fine curls of his hair. Then she gestured to Vaughn to return the joint. He hesitated, rolling the paper between thumb and forefinger.

"Take a hit," she told him.

He shook his head and passed it to her outstretched hand.

"Were you always such a puritan?"

"I don't need it."

"But James does. You've set a very bad example for your son. He's wound so tight I keep waiting for the last twist that will make him explode. Shards of James flying in all directions."

Vaughn gestured toward the baby now breathing softly on his mother's chest. "Is he really James' son?"

"Don't you mean really your grandson?"

"It's the same thing."

"Technically."

"Well?"

She brought the joint to her lips, sucked a deep hit, and emitted the smoke with a hiss through her teeth. Vaughn took it as a gesture of mockery.

"James is much more his mother's child," she said.

He felt a throb of real anger. "What has that got to do with it?"

"He's afraid of me. You must know that. He taps on the door to my room, whispers my name, and then waits. It's like begging. Maybe he should try marching right in."

"And then what?"

"We'd have to find out, wouldn't we?"

Vaughn wanted to slap the joint from her fingers, slap the expression off her face.

To his surprise, she reached the baby out to him, the boy dangling from her hands, his face quivering as if about ready to release a wailing. For an instant Vaughn was ready to stand up and walk away, but he leaned forward and accepted the child, gripped him under his arms and pulled him up to his shoulder, one hand cushioning his padded bottom, The wetness had seeped through the diaper into the fleece of the bunting. He knew he could return the boy to Claudine in a manner that would rebuke her mothering. But he wrapped him tighter, felt the child relax in his grip, the red curls brushing under his chin. He touched fingertips to the boy's face, felt the warm flesh.

"Grandpa," she said.

"Am I?" He wanted to love the child, sure he would tremble with a rush of emotion if she said yes.

"Then," she said, "we would have a real connection. A permanent one."

"Don't we?" The baby gulped and emitted a strand of white spittle that ran down Vaughn's throat.

Claudine didn't answer. She closed her eyes and lay back on the grass, stretched her arms wide, and flicked away the stub of the joint. Vaughn stared down at her face trying to read her emotions but found only an opaque calm.

He leaned forward to place the baby on her, bracing himself with a hand that came down in the rich red hair fanned behind her head, his fingers tangled in the strands. Her expression did not change. Her eyes did not flutter. Still he suspected she knew what he was doing. He wondered what would happen if he yanked on her hair, if he twisted it in his fist. But he didn't. He just stayed as immobile as she and waited for her to move first.

THE LILIES OF WOLF CREEK
Susan Tekulve

Near dawn, Dean Sypher watched from his back porch as his daughter ran through half light toward the game trail leading from his house to Wolf Creek, wearing a flowered summer dress, her red hair flaming behind her. Dean set his coffee down on the porch step and followed her, keeping a distance as she twisted through pitch pine and briar, dropping down a clay steep, reaching the bank. As his daughter slid the canoe into the creek, Dean stood on the bottomland above the bank, scouting downstream. It was late July. Oaks and poplars towered over the water, bending beneath a summer's weight of ivy and moss. Mist rose from the eddies, brimming above laurel overhanging the limestone ledges on both sides of the stream. Beneath the mist, a black otter worked the sand bank, pulling the debris of two week's rain from the water, dragging it beneath a tree toppled by an outer current. The wind played rough above the squirrelly rapids. Dean waved his arms, pointing toward the water, calling out, "It's not the same as you remember it."

Hannah paused but did not look back. She stepped into the craft, pushed off and knelt in the center. The boat rocked and settled beneath her delicate weight. Dean scrambled over two boulders as she pried her paddle's blade through mist and water. Along the left bank, a wave chain unfurled, spilling over gold and copper stones. To the right, eddies chopped and hissed across broken rocks. As Hannah steered smoothly through the chute between wave and eddy, her body disappeared into the mist, but her hair remained in sight. The red hue of it looked unearthly, like a tropical flower circling along the Amazon River, and for a moment Dean stopped worrying

35

about her safety, remembering that he'd taught her how to read water before she learned her letters. She knew how each rock moved a current, and how to let the current work for her. Her fight was not with the water. It was with him. He needed to get to the source of it. As he walked down the bank, the mist passed through him like a cold and weary hand.

Hannah's whole body reappeared at the bottom of the rapid. She dug in, allowing the eddy line to turn the boat, pulling it into shore. She stood with her feet against the bilge, perfectly balanced, and looked him directly in the eye.

"It's never been the same as you remember it," she said.

He studied her thin dress, blooming with yellow and orange poppies, her bright hair tumbling wildly around her pale face and neck. Her mother's skin, Dean thought, knowing his wife, Sadie, would have reached their daughter sooner than this. She'd already have told Hannah that she should be wearing bug spray, sunscreen, tennis shoes and a life jacket. Hannah settled her hands on her hips, another Sadie gesture that tightened his chest and knocked the air from his lungs. As she stood before him, twenty-one and motherless, his daughter seemed the hardest kind of woman to keep safe.

"The river's changing," he said.

"You mean it's dying," she said.

"It's impaired. You can't paddle all of it."

"Well," she said, moving into the bow seat, waiting for him to climb in. "You'll just have to show me how to get through the tough parts."

Dean tucked his matches and cigarettes inside his hat, stepped into the stern. A wave splashed over the left gunwale, shooting water into his left ear, deafening him.

"Water's cold," he yelled, flipping his head to shake the water out, rocking the canoe.

Hannah grasped the gunwales, steadying herself. "Don't make me a swimmer today."

"Since when did you get so girly?"

"Since you started smoking and going around Rosie's Island again."

"That old dive? I call that The Toothless Bar. Ain't a woman in it that's got all the teeth in her head."

Hannah turned on him. "I didn't say anything about the women." She glanced sharply over his chest. His ribs and breastbone tightened again, as if she could see the white scar running through his sternum. "I was talking about the smoke and the bar, and how going there might not be such a good idea with your bad heart," she said.

"It was a good bypass," he said weakly, suddenly tired of her knowing comments. How much could she really know about him? She'd been away at college the last four years. She'd come home that summer with a degree in English and Foreign Languages, without a job or money. She needed a place to stay before she went on to graduate school in Rome that fall, where she would live off a scholarship. He didn't want to charge her for board, but she insisted on paying him for her food, though she hardly ate anything. As payment, she offered to clean out her mother's belongings from the spare bedroom where Sadie lived the last year of her illness. The room had been closed off, untouched since his wife died in the cancer wing of the hospital on Good Friday. Over a year had passed since then, but Dean still stayed far away from the room, often the whole house. Most of the time, he slept in the garage or wandered over to his family's land on the next ridge to sleep in the cedar guesthouse beneath the old, empty farm house where he'd grown up.

Dean pushed off and sat in the stern seat. He steered past a friendly stone sleeping above the surface, a soft pillow of water pouring over it. Ahead, water circled and crossed a broad limb that had fallen into the channel. He had no idea what the water around it was doing. He could not see the whole river stretching beyond it.

"You can't go downstream blind," he said.

"I can see the next eddy," she said. "We can catch it and hop to the next one."

"You want to know what the water is doing. You need to put yourself in a position to see."

"I can see far enough. We can read the rest of it on the fly."

"If it's easy enough," he said.

"Is there ever an easy thing?"

37

Dean wondered when his daughter had become so fearless and unpredictable, her moods changing swiftly from cool to hostile to quietly resolved. While Hannah cleaned out her mother's sick room, Dean had brought lamp after lamp to the room whose window remained half-lit by sun filtered through pine. "You got enough light?" he asked every time he brought another lamp, lingering in the doorway, amazed and almost angered by the ease with which his daughter packed up her mother's belongings. Hannah's face softened, but she never once cried as she folded Sadie's cotton house dresses into grocery bags, topping the dresses with bars of herbal soap carved into shapes of flowers, still wrapped in cellophane. Dean had bought the loose dresses after Sadie's skin began burning from all the radiation, when she couldn't stand the touch of her own clothes. She'd thought the flowered soaps too pretty to open. Hannah had come home on weekends to help him take care of her mother, but she didn't live through the day and night rituals of her mother's illness. Dean guessed she must have seen the dresses and soaps as small gifts given to comfort the sick who had no hope of being well again. There was nothing in the room that had belonged to her mother when she was healthy, nothing to dredge up hazardous memories. Dean had left his daughter alone to finish packing the room, dimly shamed, wondering what he'd been so afraid of finding in it.

"Which way? Hannah asked. They'd come up on an island that forked the river into two waterways. To the right, the currents poured around a souse hole, waves curling back under it. To the left, a bridge hung above the channel, thin as fishing filament, its pilings glinting silver with paint from other aluminum canoes that had been drawn to it.

"Right," he said, noticing too late the faded skull and cross bone flag on the right bank. It was Rosie's joke, a secret signal she hung out on the island whenever her liquor license expired and she still wanted to stay open. The bar was an old homestead patched by salvaged lumber and tires, hidden just inside the trees. When the rangers came around to fine fishermen and campers to make up for state cuts in their revenue, Rosie took down her flag, moved her establishment to a different island, another abandoned homestead. Wherever the bar floated to, you could only row or swim to it.

The sun flickered through spikes of skinny black pines on the bank of the island, and Dean felt guilty for telling Hannah that all the women at the bar were toothless. He wanted to holler out for Rosie, the bar's proprietor, to catch their rope and haul them the rest of the way in. Rosie had a good set of teeth. She kept a jar of Dean's favorite mustard in the bar's fridge and named a country ham sandwich after him, the Sypher Special. Widowed the same year as Dean, Rosie had been set up with 96 acres, two condos in Pigeon Forge, a red Dodge truck and a John Deere tractor by her lawyer husband, though he'd left her childless. She ran the bar to ease her loneliness, claiming that her patrons were better than any of the bereavement groups offered by local churches. Dean agreed with her. Who wanted to sit around talking about their dead spouses in a church basement? When they'd discussed Hannah's drifty behavior since she'd come back, Rosie had smoked philosophically over a glass of Old Crow.

"It's only the grief," she said. "When a child loses a parent, she'll usually start acting like one or the other. If Hannah acts all ornery, like you, she won't have to think of Sadie, the sweet one. She won't have to let go of her mother."

"You don't think I'm sweet?" Dean joked.

"You have your kind moments, but sweetness isn't your nature. Sadie was the nice one." She tapped the ash of her cigarette into his empty glass, adding absentmindedly, "Saint Sadie. You know I saw her once in church, when I was still going. I turned around, and she was right behind me, and I thought, 'Now that's the saddest-faced woman I ever saw.' "

Rosie's comments had stung. At the time, Dean remembered, he'd hoped her teeth would rot out of her head for saying that he wasn't the nice one, for implying that he'd made his wife into a sad-faced woman pitied by strangers in church. He hadn't been back to see Rosie since that conversation. Now, he guessed her words hurt because they were partly true. Sadie was the nice one. His shy, easy-going wife would not have wished for a friend to lose all her teeth, no matter how angry or hurt the friend made her feel.

The water became easy for a while, so they worked harder paddling. The mist evaporated in open sunlight, and Dean began to look forward to the rapids, the cooling buffer of water and wind between himself and his daughter. He felt glad to be in the guiding seat, where he could see what the rocks were forcing the water into, the patterns on the river, and what the patterns on the top meant about the bottom of the river and what they were coming up on. In the calm places, Hannah swirled her hands in the icy current, as she had when she was younger. Her wrists were still thin as a child's, so tiny he could wrap his thumb and forefinger around them. She held her head just over the side, letting the tips of her hair trail in the water, leading him to ponder why she'd darkened her auburn hair into such an unnatural shade of red.

The week she came home and started cleaning her mother's room, Dean remembered finding a red stain around the bathtub drain. Panic shot through him as he rummaged the medicine cabinet, searching for razor blades, suspecting a sad and messy business. When he confronted her about the stain, she'd shown him a box of henna powder she'd used to dye her hair. He thought of his daughter's daily shots of Jack Daniel's she drank from tiny bottles she kept in her purse, the way she stayed up all night reading Dante's *Inferno* in Italian. Once, he'd asked her to read aloud to him from the book, and she'd read, "nulla speranza li conforta mai,/ non che posa, ma di minor pena." The words sounded so beautiful that he asked if he could tape record her, but she laughed, saying that she'd just read from the fifth canto, where the lustful were forever buffeted by violent storms. Then, she translated what she'd just read, "There is no hope that ever comforts them—no hope for rest and none for lesser pain." Dean guessed she needed to be out here on this water for the same reason she needed to henna her hair and speak Italian, drink those whiskey miniatures. He would stay here with his benumbed daughter, try to buffer her from the violent currents of her unspoken grief.

Though she'd never said so, he knew Hannah believed he hadn't protected her mother enough. He should have forced her to go to the hospital sooner, but he'd promised Sadie she could stay in her own bed as long as she wanted, beneath a window that overlooked the mountain. How tough his wife had been, enduring more pain than anyone he'd ever known, even when the cancer moved from her breasts into her spine, flaking bones that spiked her spinal cord with her every movement. She would not go into the hospital, claiming she didn't want to die drugged in an anonymous gray room. When the cancer spread into her pelvis, snapping it in two, she still would not go. He took the snowplow off his truck, readying it for the drive over the mountain to the hospital, but she'd simply shaken her head, "Not yet." Crazed by his wife's pain, he'd run down the game trail in the middle of a spring snowfall and broken the skin of ice over the creek. Wading in, he stood among rocks topped by five inches of snow, let the freezing water pierce his ankles, imagining himself under snowy quilts, making love to all the women he'd known, each one younger than Sadie, bewitching him on the brass bed of the little guesthouse where he often took them. As his wife lay in the house on the hill above him, quietly enduring a pain he could not imagine, all the women he remembered became faceless but with healthy bodies, both their breasts intact, their pelvises unbroken. He'd never strayed from his wife during the last two years of her life, during her illness. As he recalled himself standing in the winter creek, numbing himself with thoughts of other women, he felt completely faithless.

The boat approached a calm pool of water. A steel beam bridge hung over a line of quiet water running across the entire width of the creek. Beyond the line, he knew, was a blasted mill dam. What used to be an eight foot, solid wall was now a one-hundred-yard stretch of broken concrete, jagged rocks shredding the scrolling water until it was unreadable. He steered the boat to the shore, searching for a take out.

"We need to scout this one," he said.

They walked the scouting trail and looked out over the rapids. The rocks bit at the water, forming waves upon waves devouring each other, pouring into foaming holes that could hold a boat under and keep it there. He saw a whole fallen chestnut leaning against the top of the ruined dam, its roots reaching skyward, as if it had grown upside down in the middle of the falls. He nodded toward the uprooted tree, the dry boulder garden at the end of the rapid. "We'll have to portage this part," he said.

Dean shouldered the canoe, tucking his head inside, keeping the boat high enough to see the trail. Hannah walked ahead, carrying the paddles. They climbed up stone stairs that ended before they reached the burned-down

41

grist mill. They stepped carefully over the petrified tree roots that veined the dirt around the long flat lime stones that once formed the mill's foundation. Somebody had built a bonfire on top of the limestone, using the spokes of the old overshot wheel. The charred remains crawled with soiled condoms and empty beer bottles.

"Wasn't this the mill village?"

"It's past," Dean said, urging her forward.

The locusts droned, and the canoe trapped heat beneath it, and he had to set the canoe down gently every few yards. He glanced back over their difficult run, longing for chill mist and rapids. A white heron stood in the shallows, still as an ice sculpture, hunting the low current that trickled around the dry stones. Dean willed Hannah to look back with him, to take comfort in the beauty of the heron, the patterns of water falling over the mill dam. Hannah turned away, staring down at the sordid remains scattered over the charred grist mill. She pulled her hair into a loose ponytail. Dean noticed a black square, the size of two postage stamps, on the back of her neck. Believing it was a piece of wet bark, he reached out to wipe it off, but it would not come off. He wiped again and looked closer, saw a square of slender, black bars burned into her skin.

"What have you done to yourself?"

"It's a bar code."

"Why a bar code?" he asked. "How could you do this to your pretty skin?" Your mother's skin.

"It's my price."

"You're too young to have one," he said, meaning the tattoo.

"Everybody's got a price. What's yours?"

"I never had a price."

"Yours was expensive, but she always paid it."

Dean felt as he had when she'd read to him about hell in Italian. Her talk of human currency seemed as mystifying as any foreign language, though the drift of her meaning was far from beautiful. He felt tired and unschooled, bewildered by her quiet anger at him, her refusal to find hope or any comfort in the water and woods.

42

"Is this how they taught you to talk at college?" he said. "Because if it is, you just wasted a whole lot of time and money. I don't understand a word of what you just said. I wish you would talk straight, and tell me why you've been giving me hell all day."

He sat on the overturned canoe, letting his heel bang against its side more violently than he intended. The trash-can echo startled the white heron. It flapped its lanky wings, its flight ungainly as it rose slowly and bounced on a cypress limb. Hannah didn't flinch. She sat down on the canoe and pulled a bottle out of her dress pocket, setting it between them. At first, he mistook it for one of the whiskey miniatures she kept in her purse. Then he saw that the glass was filled with a strong pink liquid that changed color as she held it up in the light, its pink deepening into orange then red.

"Who did this nail polish belong to?" she asked.

"It was your mother's."

"She never wore color."

"She usually didn't."

"Then why was it in her bedroom? Why was it in the drawer of her bed stand?"

"She thought her feet looked ugly," Dean said. "That's the reason she gave for not wanting to go into the hospital sooner. She didn't want the doctors to see her ugly feet. When it got so bad, I bought that nail polish for her so that she could paint her toenails. It was the only way I could get her to go."

Hannah stared at him, disbelieving. "You owed her," she said. "You could have at least waited until after she was gone to start up again."

He tried to explain why Sadie, his shy wife who wore no makeup and refused to dye her hair, was struck by a sudden case of vanity at the very end of her life. He tried to explain his trip to the New Graham Pharmacy, how he'd left the safety of aisles stocked with eyeglasses and heating pads, turning into the treacherous cosmetic section, passing picture after picture of women with their heads tilted back, lips parted, as if waiting to be kissed above the shelves of bottles filled with jade, red and copper polish, their names more head-spinning than their bright colors—Ocean Love Potion, Cherish,

43

Autumn Promise. He'd put a bottle of each kind of polish into his basket and took them all home, spilling the bottles on the bed beside her. She picked out the deepest pink, Caliente Coral. As she leaned forward to paint her toes, she winced, and he took the bottle from her hands. "Let me." His hands shook, but she spoke to him until his hand steadied and he could finish the first coat, blowing gently over it, starting on the second. Kneeling at his wife's feet, painting slowly and carefully, he felt like he was repeating a powerful prayer or chant.

"It helped her," he said.

Hannah had already turned and walked away from him, toward the end of the creek. She slipped through a marshy patch of cattails that thickened and arched over the shoal. On the other side of the marsh, a mountain formed at the confluence of Wolf Creek and a newer river, the first slope unfolding from the shoals, rising into green waves of grass dotted by outcroppings of red picnic tables. Above the picnic tables, orange lilies ran across the hillside, clinging to the bluffs. Bright kayaks and canoes crowded the new river, sending safe, uniform ripples across its surface. Hannah had no interest in paddling it. Dean found her sitting on the bank. When he reached her, she bummed a cigarette from him, and he shook one from the pack he'd hidden beneath his hat.

"It's a strong color," she said. "I can see how it would have helped her."

Encouraged, Dean nodded toward the bright lilies on the slope. "The old timers used to make a wine from them that had an odd effect," he said. "After two or three glasses, a man saw dreams that had a great power and beauty, but in the morning he always felt like he'd committed a terrible crime."

He lit a match, and Hannah cupped her hand around the flame he offered. She lay back on the bank, looking like something beautiful and expensive, dredged from the water's silted depths. Her bright dress blended with the dark grass and white clover. Her red hair glowed, sun-streaked and deepening as it swirled wildly around her face and throat. The threat of blush or sunburn lingered just beneath the delicate surface of her white skin.

She'd crossed her forearm over her chest, and she fell asleep balancing the cigarette expertly between her fingers. Eyes closed, her smile remained a secret. He'd never know what she remembered about his marriage to her mother, or if she believed there'd been any kind moments between them. That was her price, and he'd keep paying it. He sat beside her, reaching to take the burning cigarette from her fingers before its ashes could drop, but he put down his hand, afraid of waking her. A black shadow slipped down the mountain, exposing the soft green summit. The hazy summer sky billowed like a starched sheet chafing all that lay bare and devoted beneath it.

RUBY-IN-A-BOTTLE

Renée Ashley

So now only a withdrawn horizon can take her & will–your attraction is natural She is the red shift's shadow & her hours are fractal & full Oh we each fall–mad for her–on our filthy knees (who can resist someone who does not care) But she is neither love-apple nor rosy cheek She's not ruby-captured-in-a-bottle not slip-of-a-knife not hummingbird's throat Neither plum blossom nor the heart of a doe descending a slope She is nothing you'll get to know Are you listening You're not listening Listen Throw your puny arms around this one & you'll end up standing–every awestruck nickle of you–between the piss and the awful bloody pot of her indifference You are looking for a nice redheaded girl A little something to capture Something gravid with unknowing and heat Oh you're looking for something–admit it–on fire So there she is She's the head of a match she's the tip of a star she's the sun she's the whole goddamn Milky Way & she's spiraling past you She is everywhere You can't hold her That's crazy You're crazy Look You could kiss her from here

MY RED DESDEMONA
David R. Poe

She was standing at the top of the stairway in La Gare, the restaurant where my troupe of players and I were about to celebrate the finale of *Hamlet*, our offering that August for Shakespeare in the Bois. La Gare was an old train station, and we were seated right where the tracks would have been, now covered over in fine oak planks. There were maybe a dozen of us, and I, as their director, was determined to lead us into a riotous night of food and drink. As hot a night as it was, the terrace to the rear of the station, down the tracks, was shut, because of an impending storm. They had left the doors open for the air, and you could smell the rain coming.

I don't know how many times I looked up at the red-haired woman, but I realized she was searching the platforms below, as a woman years earlier might, waiting for someone to arrive. I had not seen Sheila in at least twenty years, and at first I thought her appearance here in Paris, at the top of those stairs, an improbable coincidence. But the more I looked the more I realized it was her. La Gare was immense, cavernous, and to muffle the crowd noise thick sheets of white cloth hung from the girders. I made her out—some fifty feet away—between two of these sheets. She herself wore white, a summery, sleeveless dress, and all that whiteness made her orange long hair all the more shocking. She seemed anxious, like a woman waiting for her lover.

"Hey, Joe," someone asked me, "Cote du Rhone okay with dinner?"

"Sure." I rose and stared at her. She saw me. Then turned and walked away. "Excuse me," I said and rushed after her.

The last time I had seen Sheila was during a cold Upstate winter. We were in amateur theater, she acting, I directing, and we lived together in an attic atop an old Victorian house. The attic formed an A-frame, but the wood was unfinished and uninsolated, and between the joists the points of the nails holding down the shingling outside poked through old brown slats. There was one cast iron radiator that clanged and hissed. From the high roof beam I had hung a swing, and we were always warning visitors who wanted try it out —often drunk or high—not to get a face or butt full of nails.

We were rehearsing *Othello* at the small Salt City Theater, a few blocks from our attic. Sheila played Desdemona. Her red hair and fair freckled skin made her unusual for the part, since in those looks one might expect a fiery Maureen O'Hara, which in turn made Sheila's subtle innocence seem all the more confounding. Our Othello was played by Ahmad, from the Bronx, a big black guy with a thunderous voice, ideal for the Moor in Shakespeare's eyes. The Bard was a bit blind when it came to geography, but he just had to have the ram tupping the ewe be black. That night we finished rehearsal about five-thirty. I had a dinner date with my father at six at his favorite steak house, to talk business, that being his business, heating and air-conditioning. I told Sheila I would meet her back at the attic, and walked off into a blustery February evening, thinking of how we would keep each other warm that night under our big down quilt. About halfway to the restaurant, maybe five blocks, I realized I had left my calculator in the director's office at the theater. I hurried back. The side door we used was locked, but I had my own key. Inside, I flipped on a light to a corridor leading to the back stage area. Before I reached the office, I heard voices. They came from the room where we stored props and what modest scenery the theater could afford. The voices were low, throaty, incoherent. I turned a corner into darkness and saw a flickering light escaping from a partly opened door. By now I knew what the human sounds meant. I slid quietly along the wall, until I reached the door. I looked in. There on a bed—the Desdemona death bed—lay Ahmad, supine and naked, his feet on the floor, his dark body barely visible. A candle had been lit, the most bitterly ironic candle in all of theater. "Put out the light, and then put out the light." Kneeling on the floor between Ahmad's legs was Sheila, her red hair and white skin impossibly radiant.

For years afterward I reflected on that moment, wishing I had been capable of a mighty Shakespearean rage. Instead, I slipped away silently, holding the fury and pain inside. Indeed, there was a greater influence at work that night, more massive than jealousy. My father. Who was not the kind of man you cancelled a business dinner with. I ran to the attic, pulled out a suitcase, and stuffed in everything of mine that I could. I thought about slashing the ropes of the swing, but the ladder I had used to hang it was hidden away in the cellar. Outside, the snow fell harder and pelted my face, flakes melting and mixing with tears. I caught my breath outside the restaurant. By the time I actually entered, I was forty minutes late and surprised to see my father calmly going over computer printouts and biding my tardiness. A Tuesday night, slow, my father had taken over a table meant for six. I approached. Looking up, he said, "I thought we agreed on six." He studied my face, read the obvious, then allowed himself to see my suitcase.

"She fucked you over, didn't she. I'm not surprised." I sat down, and he called Beverly over, our usual waitress, and ordered big, like we had something to celebrate. Two sixteen-ounce Porterhouses, rare, a bottle of Dewar's and a small bucket of ice. "You'll get over it. A man can get over anything. "

He showed me plans, projections for his move south into the mid-Atlantic seaboard. Spread sheets, numbers, graphs, my father's incessant tapping of his pen on the rim of his glass, bites of near raw meat—it helped my head. But the image, her red hair, was burnt into my chest.

"Where's your calculator?"

"I left it at the theater."

"Christ, almighty. Texas Instruments. Best they got. Make sure you collect it with the rest of your stuff. Tomorrow." He saw a split with Sheila as a split with theater. Something he had no use for, unless it meant a building he could equip with a compressor, fans and air ducts. It was my mother's love of theater that had led to amusement for my sister but infection for me. She took us to local plays, and later, on train trips to New York City, Broadway,which lit up at night like a carnival, a million miles from our hometown. My father had no use for Sheila either, though he had met her only a few times, briefly. She was from Long Island, "Something hanging from an ass that thinks it wags the dog."

49

"We'll set you up outside DC, along the I-270. It'll be the biggest industrial corridor on the east coast in three years." He mopped away some bloody juice with a piece of bread. "You know, maybe the old suspicion is true. Redheads have no souls. So they try to suck the soul out of you. You finally see that, Joe?" He knocked back the last shot of scotch. "A man can get over anything."

A few years after that dinner, my mother died of pancreatic cancer. The day after the funeral a Salvation Army truck arrived and took away her clothes. I had to get back to DC to oversee the heat and air in a renovated theater on Fifteenth Street.

I thought less and less often of Sheila. But it amazed me how often the attic rose up in my dreams, as if it had pyramidal powers. Even two decades later I still dreamed of the attic, several times a year. The space was always shifting, different levels, different planes, like a stage set, all made in wood, and clearly within the A-frame. So often I would see the swing and at first Sheila would be seated in it, going back and forth. I think she was happy. But slowly she disappeared from the dreams. And I never dreamed of her at Desdemona's bed, with Ahmad, though often, early on, waking from my attic dream, my mind would collide with that memory, her white skin, the movement of her head, her red hair. But even that memory had seemed to have faded out by the time I saw Sheila standing at the top of the staircase, peering onto the platforms, in a station with a pitched ceiling, all of which seemed itself a variation on our attic.

I ran up the steps and into the bar. It had the same brick walls from years ago when it was the entrance to the station, no doubt with ticket counters, maps, a newsstand. Now it was chic, softly lit, with a zinc bar and tables where people met before going downstairs to eat. I saw Sheila standing by the door, looking out. The forecasted rain had arrived, in blinding sheets. She couldn't get out, and when she turned I was standing before her.

"Hello, Sheila."

She acted confused. "*Pardon?*" she said, the French way.

"Sheila, it's me. Joe."

"*Qui? Est-ce-que je vous connais* ? "

I could connect the dots and remember. The freckles on her forehead and cheeks, constellations I had once memorized, like a budding astronomer.

"Sheila, I know it's you."

Finally, she cleared her throat. "I didn't know if I would be able to talk to you." She looked young. So much so it scared me. "I followed you after the show. You still head for nearest bar. I'd seen your name on a poster in a bookshop. *Hamlet*. Directed by Joe Dunn." It had been at least half an hour before we left the theater, which meant she had to wait somewhere, and remember.

"Not exactly a billboard in Times Square or Piccadilly Circus."

"It was a good show, Joe."

"It was what it was."

La Gare was normally packed, but the weather was keeping customers away. I found a table, she followed, and we settled into low seats, padded, swiveling. A waitress swept in, clearing away debris, giving the surface a wipe and asking what we wanted. Sheila ordered chardonnay and I ordered Dewar's on the rocks. Lovers-meeting -after-twenty-years. What a strange scene to play, because it couldn't possibly matter, couldn't possibly change anything.

"So," I said, "where were we?"

She swiveled, and her legs cleared the table, one crossed over the other, her dress pulling back above the knee. "As I recall, you made a sudden exit. I don't think it was in the script."

"I'm sorry. Was that an exit left? Right? Or did I simply drop through the floor? I forget."

"I figured your father's strangle hold had finally gotten to you. He probably had you evacuated by private helicopter."

Had she no idea what I'd seen? I laughed. Should I be bent on making her acknowledge the truth? The waitress brought the drinks.

"Sheila, I saw you. Do you understand? I went back to the theater. I had forgotten something."

She looked at me strangely and sipped her wine. "Honestly, Joe. I don't know what you're thinking." Her voice rose a bit. "I only know I went back to our place and you were gone. Your things. Jesus, Joe, you even cut down the swing."

"I never cut down the swing."

"Yes, you did, Joe. You did."

I leaned into her face, spoke low, almost growling. "I never cut down the swing."

"Upon my knees, what does your speech import? I understand a fury in your words, but not the words."

"Sheila, don't play. Who cares now? Who cares? Why lie?"

"To whom, my Lord? With whom? How am I false?"

"Stop, Sheila."

"Alas, the heavy day! Why do you weep? Am I the motive of these tears, my lord?" She brushed a finger across each of my cheekbones.

"Bravo. Okay, okay. 'What? Not a whore?'"

"You left, Joe, and I never knew why. You hurt me."

"Is't possible?"

"I loved you, Joe. How many times did we tell each other?"

"I cry you mercy, then: I took you for that cunning whore of Venice."

She carefully set her glass down. "At least my father wasn't my pimp." In one breath, she admitted whorishness and accused me of the same.

"What does it matter, Sheila? We were together six months. That's twenty-year-old blood under the bridge. "

"I know. The stream moves on. Now you're married. French wife. Two kids. Boy and a girl. When you're the son-slash-partner at Dunn Air and Heat, you become Google worthy, not to mention head of European operations. You air-condition the Eiffel Tower yet?" She spoke a little too jovially, an old buddy proud of what I'd done in life.

"Did you also read my old man died? A year ago, almost to the day."

"They only said, suddenly." Yeah, I thought, no details. Not allowed. Which was good.

There was someone standing beside our table. A young couple, dripping wet, both in blue jeans, him with a Yankee baseball cap, her with hair done up in braids and beads.

"You're Joe Dunn, the director, aren't you?"

"I suppose I am."

The girl spoke up, gushing. "We just wanted to say how great the production was." They were Brits.

"Yes," the boy jumped in. "Excellent. We're in theater, too." Then they fluttered off and squeezed in at the bar.

I laughed. "See, the critics are raving."

"Like I always told you, the next Lee Strasbourg."

I looked at the kid with the Yankee cap. Ahmad had worn one of those, too, always bragging about his Bronx Bombers.

"So, aren't you going to ask why *I'm* in Paris?" Her green eyes bubbled up.

"A zillion visitors each year. Why not you?"

"My oldest daughter starts Beaux Arts in a few weeks. I'm moving her in, helping her set up house."

As good as I was in math, I couldn't imagine the addition. "That means at least two daughters. Well. Life does go on."

"I'd like to tell you all about it." She had worked her chair around and her knee touched mine. "I'm at the Hotel Saint Martin. Nice view on the canal. My daughter's staying with her future roommates. Come spend some time with me." She leaned across and kissed me on the lips. "You remember how good we were?"

"Apparently not good enough."

"Honestly, Joe, I don't know what you're thinking."

"I can't compartmentalize like you."

"Everybody compartmentalizes. I hear the French are good at it. A spouse here, a lover there." She rubbed her hand along my arm. "Aren't you the least bit curious? Can't you just imagine?" Imagination. Memory. They seemed to curl up into one. Her apricot smell—now as it had been then. The thick long hair. The opalescent skin held together by freckles. She rose, drew a breath, sighed. "Just imagine, Joe." She bent and kissed me again. "Hotel Saint Martin, three nights." She walked toward the door. Suddenly, she stopped and turned.

"You know something, Joe. I still have dreams of the attic, even now, after all these years. You ever dream of the attic?"

"Don't be daft."

"And Joe, you did cut down the swing." She sashayed out, into the night. The rain had stopped, and the streetlights made a glow she disappeared into.

I'd lied. More than once. When you are the director of Dunn Air and Heat, Europe, it's easy to compartmentalize. And when I'd been on the road for a week or two and returned home to my wife, kissing her hello, sweeping up the kids in hugs, I'm sure she compartmentalized as well. The swing? I honestly couldn't remember cutting it down. I had thought about it, that I remembered. Memory and imagination. For sure there are certain images I would always remember. My red haired Desdemona with her Othello, for one.

I looked at my watch. After midnight. One year to the day. There are also images you remember but have only imagined. I imagined my father in a strange arid land, driving a truck on his way to double check the finishing touches on the biggest job Dunn Air had ever known, when suddenly the truck blows up, and he doesn't get out. The day before, I had heard from him. He said the airport job at Basra was nearly done and we were up a quarter mill. But he was sitting on four thousand window units. "It's 121 degrees today. They drive around in their cars to keep cool. Can't afford a lousy window unit for the house. Plus the electric shortage. The heat never stops. No wonder so many blow themselves up. Must be cooler in paradise. Hey, how bout it! –Dunn Air, Paradise Division. Virgins not included. I luv ya, Joe."

"Hey, Joe, Joe, where you been?" I turned to see our Horatio. "You up for this? You OK?" He put his hand on my shoulder, squeezed. "Maybe this wasn't a good idea."

"Ah, Horatio, there is a divinity that shapes our ends." I took a sip of Dewar's. "I'll be down in a minute."

"Sure, Joe. You take your time."

I thought about ordering another drink. They would understand my

54

need to be alone. They might not understand my need to lose myself in her red hair, scan every inch of her skin. I left a twenty on the table and went to find a cab, fleeing one ghost in search of another.

LAUGHTER IN THE DARK

Niels Hav

One woman is enough
to drive a whole neighborhood crazy.
Anyhow all traffic lights turned red
when you walked home from the laundromat
with your delicates.

I'd just gone inside to write
a poem in dry weather; and now I stand here
tyrannized by ambulances
and hysteria while the sky turns dark
out over the lakes. Come on!

Translated from the Danish by Thomas E. Kennedy

OTHER PEOPLE'S PROBLEMS
Ladette Randolph

The young woman drove a red Mazda. She stopped at the gas station on Highway 2 on a Monday afternoon. The attendant told her it was a full-service station, and while she used the restroom, he filled the tank, washed her windshield, checked the oil and the pressure in the tires.

She smiled when he told her everything was fine. "You don't find service like this just every day," she said, adding, "I hope you're right though, that everything's fine."

She was a pretty woman, not really young, but not old either. She wore her red hair in a haphazard pony tail, and she was outfitted in a T-shirt and cropped cargo pants. On her left hand, she wore a large diamond in a thick wedding band.

"How far you heading tonight?" the attendant asked.

Maybe she startled a little too much at the question, paused a second too long before answering, "Not far," she finally said, offering nothing more than that. Her earlier openness shifted. Her eyes seemed weary and wary.

She paid, said thank you and drove off. The attendant would have thought nothing more about her if the next day an older man hadn't come through late in the afternoon. The man was dressed casually, but he carried himself with confidence, like he'd once been an athlete and was now the chairman, or director, or head of something.

While he was paying for his gas, the man casually drew out a photograph from his wallet. It was the photograph of a woman, a very glamorous, beautiful red-haired woman, not like any one the attendant had ever seen in real life.

"Have you by chance seen this woman?"

The attendant immediately shook his head no. "I'd remember if I had." He looked at the man. "She your wife?"

The man looked at the photograph and his expression hardened a little. "Yes."

Before leaving, the man said, "She drives a little red Mazda." At this, the attendant brought his head up quickly, but the man didn't seem to notice. The man returned to the counter and left a phone number. "You see her, give me a call." He looked at the attendant. "She's a danger to herself."

The attendant was a young man, newly engaged to be married. He'd always been an honest man, and he'd been fortunate in his life never to have been put in the middle of anything. He'd never had to decide what was true and what wasn't true. Those things had been laid out well in his mind.

He believed in telling the truth about what he knew, but a feeling he couldn't quite describe kept him from speaking up and telling the man he'd seen his wife. And then the man was gone, and the moment was lost, and the attendant told himself it was okay. He shouldn't get involved in business that wasn't his. He threw away the phone number, too, to emphasize the rightness of his decision.

That evening as he ate dinner at his fiancee's parent's house, he couldn't stop thinking about things. He watched his future in-laws. They were friendly and familiar, and he'd never thought of them apart from one another. He looked at his fiancee, also friendly and familiar. A nice girl, wholesome, innocent as could be, and he felt engulfed by a familiar feeling of tenderness and protectiveness that he understood as love. What would he think if she left and hadn't told him where she was going? He couldn't imagine such a thing. She told him every move she made. Sometimes more than he wanted to know.

This was what bothered him, though, the not knowing. If the wife had left, and she was a danger to herself, wouldn't he have noticed something? Was she running away for a reason? Oh, he didn't like feeling caught up in the drama, but he also didn't know how to lay it aside, how to live easily with it. Marriage suddenly made no sense at all.

His fiancee's mother interrupted him. "Did you want more potatoes?"

He shook his head and smiled. She said, "You must have had a hard day today. You look tired."

"I'm fine," he said. "Maybe I'll take a second helping after all."

She smiled and passed the bowl. Beneath the table, his fiancee laid her soft white hand on his thigh.

DANGER
Pamela Painter

I know you followed me with your ever-present camera the first few times I left you to be alone to read the remaining few pages, the last paragraph, the final lines of a book. Several of those books are even in the photographs you took of me as I slipped into another world. I remember where I was as I neared the end of the new translation of Madame Bovary. I would leave you to walk to a bustling café where no one knew me, order a double espresso or a Champagne Kir, and begin the ride toward the end of a dark novel or the stories of Roberto Bolano. I remember which bench I chose along the Champs-Elysees, the Jardins des Tuileries, or which table at the Café de Flore, never in the Bibliotheque Nationale, whose cool underground floors seemed meant only for my dusty archival work. Often I sat beside the fountains near the Centre Pompidou, where slowly I grew fond of its resemblance to an installation of outlandish outdoor plumbing. The books and I were in your photographs until I dissuaded you from following me by putting down my book to cover or to pin up what you called "my volcanic flow of red, red hair."

And now, I am leaving Paris, leaving you, and going home. It has taken me three weeks to divest myself of all that I acquired when I moved here a year ago for my research. Soon after we met, you tagged along with me, taking photographs as I bought tables, chairs, dishes, piece by piece, mostly at the Marche de Montreuil, and that is how—piece by piece--I set it all free.

When you complained about my leaving you to read, I tried to explain how I both love and loathe the end of a book coming on, the last pages thinning to fifteen or ten or two. It is the fingertips' tactile sense and foretells of revelation together with a disengagement, one that produces melancholy or surprise, relief or joy—a sensation that an Ipad or some other "reader" will never ever duplicate. I take pleasure in the arc of pages winging from a hard middle spine; notes made in the margins to take me back to a particular passage again and again; the slight breeze when turning each individual page.

I thought you would understand being alone, for surely your dark room, which takes up half of your miniscule apartment, is too small for the easy movements of more than one person at a time. Twice, I sat hunched in a cramped corner as you slipped photographs of me through the washes, moved them dripping wet from tray to tray. But I was really watching your cap of soft curls ride your strong neck and wide shoulders as you worked, waiting for your smile with its tiny scar on your upper lip, a white line in the mustache you sometimes coaxed along for three or four days.

We started leaving each other for different reasons months ago. Perhaps it was the evening you came over with a bottle of champagne and the announcement that you were going to have your first show. You refused to tell me any details, only that the gallery dealt mostly with contemporary British and American photographers. "Three small rooms," you said, "an intimate setting." You said the owner was a rich American who had come to Paris in the early 90s to study art and never left. His partner oversees the family vineyard in Alsace. You sounded envious.

I was disappointed when you said you didn't want me to help you hang the show. You poured more champagne into our glasses, sprinkled champagne on my three cactus plants, and said, "I want it to be a surprise."

As the date grew near, you nervously assured me that my French was good enough to get by with for the evening—as if it were a matter of language. The gallery owner, whose name had been Dave, but was now Didier, would look after me. You told me to leave my hair down, and what to wear, "that blue silk dress cut on the bias."

I said you were the first man I'd met who knew what a bias cut was.

"But it's the most flattering shape for a woman," you said. I should have heard you then—as in "any woman can wear."

We walked to the gallery, down the rue Vielle-du-Temple in the

Marais, and you warned me it would be different. "How different?" I asked. "You mean it will be something other than twenty photographs of myself strung on your clothesline, with those old-fashioned wooden clothespins our grandmothers probably used." I laughed and you said again, "It will be different from that."

As we arrived at the entrance to the brightly lit gallery, you pulled me to you, lifted my hair, and kissed my neck. And then you spread my hair around my shoulders like a cape, and said "One entire room is yours."

"But of course, you are the girl with red hair," Didier said, coming forward from a small group of people to kiss past both my cheeks. Still holding my hand, he waved you toward an older man who turned out to be his partner, then he lead me into the first room to stand before the largest photograph. I was *The Girl with Red Hair*.

The day you took that photograph, you and I had fled the heat of Paris for the gardens, pathways, and fountains of Versailles. I am lying in the late summer grass that borders the lake on the palais grounds. My favorite dress is abloom with fuchsia and golden flowers, green pointed leaves. My long hair is fanned out above my head. "Close your eyes," you said. "Touch your hair as though you were touching me," and I did, my fingers brushing my hair the way I might touch you there to begin what would surely happen next. But I never wondered what would happen the night of your show, what would happen here.

I did indeed have a room of photographs all to my unnamed self. *The Girl with Red Hair*. Didier left to greet other guests, to introduce you to your future patrons, and I moved on by myself to the next two rooms of your show. The second room was devoted to *The Girl with Shaved Head*. The third room was *The Girl Heavy with Child*.

There we were, nameless, but clearly your three women, revealed to each other. You could not resist showing your best work all at once. No wonder you did not want me here to say, "No, hang that one a little higher," or "My hair is too orange in that photograph." *The Girl Heavy with Child* was destined to become *The Girl with Child*. And indeed your child was also present in the gallery, a tiny daughter sleeping in a paisley sling against her mother's breast. Shock turned me speechless and polite, and I remember admiring the elan that only French women possess for scarves. Sharing their men is a trait that French women are thought to tolerate with the same elan. I think of the torments Simone de Beauvoir went through in spite of her professed generosity towards Sartre's young women. *The Girl with Red Hair* was not for sale. In more ways than one. I left early, alone, my hair caught up in a twist with a barrette.

I would leave the maroon couch with burns up and down its arm for the next tenant. In the bedroom where our relationship died the same night as your show, I left the mahogany headboard that needed a pillow between it-- thumping, gloriously thumping-- and the wall. The pillow will be a mystery to the next person until their own perfect night.

I put my posters from the Musee D'Orsay and Le Louvre in the hallway and tore into pieces the myriad photographs you snapped of me for almost a year, photographs so enlarged that the pixels fractured every strand of my hair."

I am thinking about endings as I pack my books, labeling the boxes to be sent home. I write my address with a black permanent marker; tape makes that static noise. Before I close the last box, I fan the pages of a several novels, unable to read their final lines. Their stories are still mine while ours is completely disengaged. I see our time together has taken on a shape with your show's revelation even as it takes on closure.

Soon I'll be back in the States, in a new place with empty rooms, waiting for the comforting arrival of my books. This morning, I carried out my three prickly cactus plants one by one, and resisted leaving signs identifying them by my pet names for them: Gustave, Collette, Martine. They sat there bare, needy, dressed only in a crayoned "Danger" sign. If this were a photograph, I would ask you to kneel beside them and place the sign on you. In some cultures it is thought that a photograph steals one's soul. If I had access to your negatives, I would steal them back. I need to forget your photographer's eye for detail, how your hand cupping the camera would lift and aim, how your eye would wander. The night of your show I knew your heart had often followed. Perhaps I'll cut my "red red" hair.

A Photo of My Mother, 1972

Steve Kowit

That's my mom on the grass with the gorgeous red hair
& her dumb cigarette. It's her before I was born. My dad,
who'd been killed in the war twelve days before
they managed to force me out of her womb, snapped
the shot. He was good at that kind of thing—
& at just about everything else, she told me, the few times
She managed to speak about him. An air force gunner
shot down over some village of huts near the end of the war.
All told, I was right not to want to come out; it would have
been best If I hadn't. I was born deaf & with half a left leg,
to add to my mom's unspeakable grief. Imagine raising
a kid by yourself who's crippled & deaf. Slaving at greasy
waitressing jobs. Stuffing tips in your pocket, scared
to death you won't make it this month. Worn down
by worry & work & no end in sight. Finding cheaper
& cheaper places to live every couple of years,
in more & more crummy sections of town. By the time
my memories start she was nothing at all of that beautiful
girl lost in dreams on the grass. & at thirty-eight she was old,
sallow, drawn, worn through. Her mouth one more grim line
on her face. Though her hair was beautiful still, her hands
shook. She smoked all the time. & coughed. She'd say
it's to keep myself calm. To get thru one more day.

She never remarried. Who'd want to take on a woman
saddled down with a deaf, crippled kid? When I was
almost eighteen, the year before she was gone, I remember
one evening signing in rage the truth that had gnawed
at my mind every day at my life, knowing from pictures
like this one, the beauty she'd been. That is to say,
I had figured out early on that I was the reason she'd never
married again. She was aghast. She shook her head
& signed back No, no that wasn't it! Absolutely that wasn't it.
Lots of guys,she signed, had been after her still. But rather,
& this I won't ever forget—we were in that last godawful
place on Lamont, with that heater that kept going dead
& windows that never closed right—that I wasn't the reason
at all. That she simply couldn't do it again. That she'd loved
my father too much. Then she hugged me & wept & fumbled
for one more of those damn cigarettes. She was already
coughing into her hands every few minutes by then, & was
gone the next winter—that gorgeous, innocent girl in the photo
sprawled out on the grass with her eyes dreamily shut & that
stream of red hair, and that beautiful skin, & that long cigarette.

FLUENT
Alexandra Marshall

I know I'm part French because I can speak it and my progressive elementary school had a theory about that. But which part of me? Not the maraschino hair that came from Galway to Manhattan with my maternal grandmother–her ticket out – along with the matching skin. The cigarette is only a prop, and anybody could buy this cheap sweater. The retro dress doesn't count either, though I let myself get talked into it, didn't I?

The theory goes that in speaking a second language a different aspect of your regular self is activated. It's the opposite of escaping into a foreign identity since you're unlocking a secret compartment within you by suddenly sensing whether a word is masculine or feminine–and if you mean *le destin* or *la destinée*–not to mention working the irregular verbs. I probably also have the mandatory intricacies of other languages stacked inside each other like wooden dolls–Gaelic for sure–but I already have enough to worry about. Here's my question: should I stay here in France?

Progressive parents may mean well, but since so many of them including mine are the product of conventional educations themselves, they don't get what it's like to grow up without governance. How smart am I when I've only ever been validated? That I'm sufficiently pretty gets confirmed every time I walk out the door, but am I reliable? I mean, am I too gullible to depend on myself?

The grass is tickling my face, making me smile. That's his plan too, along with keeping both me and the *Château de Versailles* in equal focus. It's possible that for Jacques the three dimensions are a version of the parts I'm trying to be the sum of (if you'll pardon my presumption in comparing my incomplete self to this architectural masterpiece) since, even with my eyes closed, I can see him squinting to close the gap around that boring middle distance of rented rowboats and scattered ducks. He keeps saying, "*Je t'aime*," but how much? Is *passionnément* enough?

It's my Junior Year Abroad, in other words, which means I've got someone else back home waiting for me, a pre-med with the whole rest of his life charted out like a formula that includes me as a central ingredient. His name is Jack, to create a coincidental phonic overlap that I also find annoying. Why should I have to choose who I am on the basis of a boyfriend's nationality?

I'm not the kind of girl who usually feels free to complain about my upper middle class comforts, but the equally random gift of my beauty—ask my Granny—is a fate-changer I could do without. She's had three husbands and is still going strong, though I'm not sure if the latest represents upward or downward mobility. Can you still be a trophy wife at seventy-five? To a semi-retired plastic surgeon?

Jacques only wants to rearrange me in bed, so from here we'll go back to his room in the *Cité Universitaire* where he'll again try convincing me to let him photograph me naked. He's taken me to all these galleries and museums where the unblemished women are like still-life fruit, their tinted contours seductive, but I refuse him every time until he finally quits and seduces me with his French Kisses instead. The only time I speak English with Jacques is when I'm no longer flirting, to make him understand it's time to put the camera down or else I'll pick my dress up off the floor and disappear behind a curtain of fuchsia and saffron flowers. Today I think I'll demand, "You first," and he'll have to admit, "*Touché*," relenting. Wouldn't you?

I've come to understand that Jack is simply too busy to bother trying to flatter me into submission, which isn't a fault when you consider that any day now he'll save a life with what he's learning. I'd be the first to admit that we've been quite compatible in this way, so this isn't a criticism either. It's just that I'm now wearing a black pearl around my neck on a chain so fine it's nearly invisible, a semiprecious jewel that throbs like a pulse. "It's a present from my new lover," I'd let my grandmother in on the secret if I could send home this picture, which I can't because of the cigarette that would freak my righteous parents if they knew how many people still smoke here. "Nothing," I'll answer when they ask protectively, "What was wrong with Jack?"

The difference is that 87% of the French choose to vacation in France, a statistic you can look up if you think I'm exaggerating. It's about their being so self-contained that going abroad has no appeal, an attitude I don't share or else I'd still be stuck back at NYU reading Simone de Beauvoir in English instead of discovering the footbridge named after her in Paris. "I am incapable of conceiving infinity, and yet I do not accept finity," she wrote. Other than your average Frenchman, who doesn't believe that?

I always used to wonder what I might have missed out on during any given day, but not here. Now I'm engaged to the max, body and soul, which can sometimes make me feel like a diver dropping to unsafe depths. Check your meters, you might caution me if I knew how to read them.

"You're not on drugs, are you?" my mother will ask.

"Not exactly," would be the truth, but since it's only a red wine habit I've developed, I'll settle for, "No."

"Then why won't you come home when we've sent you a ticket?"

"Because Thanksgiving isn't a holiday here? Because here it's a crime to eat a plateful of food that's all the same beige non-color?"

"What are you talking about?"

"Turkey, stuffing, gravy, the sides."

"So what?"

"It's a culinary offense."

"It's our National Meal!"

"That's what I'm talking about."

"Thanksgiving falls on my fiftieth birthday this year, Amy."

"I'm Aimée now," I correct her pronunciation.

In her sigh I can hear her stifled exasperation.

"I just got here," I'll attempt a different strategy, "so it's too soon to interrupt my momentum."

"It's already been three months."

"That's no time in a place where everything's ancient."

"The Grand Canyon is way older than Paris, so stop acting like a convert."

"A what?"

"A fanatic."

"Just because I'm finally happy?"

This stops her.

Since I'm only imagining our phone call, at least I don't have to witness the way my mom's mouth puckers up when she feels insulted or hurt. She and I aren't accustomed to arguing or even disagreeing very often, and I usually work fairly hard not to disappoint her. But surely she's aware—she's the daughter of that other immigrant redhead—that it can be a fulltime job to become independent.

"Then what about Jack?"

My "Dear John" letter will be a total lie since my not coming home has nothing to do with my academic obligations, but I'll still be shocked when Jack falls for it. I wouldn't expect him to write back "No problem" like I'm merely thanking him for having loved me, but how can all of his time be taken up with the honors version of organic chemistry? Maybe he's found a nursing student to boss around and was never interested in *égalité*. But if that's the case, why do I care?

Our meeting as freshmen was so generic that it's barely memorable, which is why our being perfect for each other (according to both sides of the aisle, so to speak) seems doubtful. I'm suspicious—aren't I descended from a wild Irish Rose?—no matter that Jack will probably always be the most decent person I'll ever know. Why this isn't enough for me is a big concern for my worried mother, but of course she's married to an insurance executive.

It's all because of how vividly I can still remember the exact moment in first grade when I performed the song like a real little French girl singing *"on y danse, on y danse"* as if I understood it referred to the famous bridge in a city I'd never heard of either. The teacher presented it as a game but we rehearsed it a lot, and the verses eventually included the vocabulary for shoemakers, musicians, soldiers, hairdressers, gardeners, and laundresses, the *beaux messieurs* and *belles dames* bowing and curtseying all the while. What I'll never forget is the thrill of the applause (in my school that wanted everyone to feel equally appreciated) singling me out as especially cute in my *début* as a *demoiselle*. Without knowing what the feeling was, I felt bilingual.

"*Viens, Aimée,*" Jacques will coax, offering a hand to pull me to my feet.

I'll comply, of course, though I already know the palace's famous Hall of Mirrors will make me dizzy. At the end of the afternoon the train back to Paris will give me another good chance to look like I'm asleep, so I'll get another opportunity to rethink everything. I'll still refuse to become Jacques's—or anybody's—nude Muse, but since I could be wrong about breaking up with Jack I probably ought to delay a final decision. And reconsider my mother's fiftieth while I'm at it.

The trouble is that Jack wants me to share his desire—his destiny— to eventually discover something as crucial as the cure for cancer. I want somebody to cure it, don't get me wrong, but what's so bad about requiring everybody to take off the month of August? Sometimes I get a little sick of the constant pressure, which is why I'm content to lie on my back like my Granny, with *rien du tout* to worry my pretty little red head about. If only I could.

GWEN, BETSY, AND ANNE-MARIE JENSEN

Dorthe Nors

A nne-Marie Jensen was born in the mid-seventies at a hospital in small-town Denmark. In Silkeborg, to be exact. She was the youngest of four children, which is important to mention here. Other things are important, too, like the fact that she enjoyed a secure upbringing in a quiet residential area of single-family homes, and that on Sundays the family often would take a picnic basket and sit down on the banks of the lake, looking out on the big hill with its viewing tower standing tall over the landscape, and that Anne-Marie always wanted to go to the top of it.

Anne-Marie did well in school, better in high school, and then moved to the capital, Copenhagen, to study the history of art. These things need to be said, along with the fact that after several successful years at Copenhagen's university, Anne-Marie decided to study a year in New York. She was fortunate enough to be admitted into Columbia's art history program, and at the same time she took on a volunteer job at one of the city's big, modern museums. All this was so that she could learn as much as possible that might take her to the top of the art world, and in that respect she was assisted in her efforts:

One of her professors at the university was Gwen Liebermann, and this Gwen Liebermann was at the same time a high-profile curator at the big, modern museum of art where Anne-Marie worked as a volunteer. About Professor Liebermann can be said that she was a middle-aged, unmarried career woman with dry skin and thin hair. Rumor had it that everything about her had withered away after a hysterectomy without the proper hormone treatment.

"She crackles like parchment when you shake her hand, but she has something..." Anne-Marie told a Danish friend over the phone, adding that Professor Liebermann was highly respected both as a member of faculty and more generally in museum circles. Basically, she was a *name* in academia.

"Ambition is no bad thing," Anne-Marie told her friend, and after that she made sure to stick close to Professor Liebermann, who seemed like someone who could pave a way for her in the world she so much wanted to be a part of.

Things went well in New York. Anne-Marie was good at her work, and she went about it with a happy Danish smile, conscientious and easygoing in everything she did. She was talented, perservering and devoted. She was ambitious, too, and one day she asked Professor Liebermann if she would be her supervisor on a paper she was writing on Mannerism. Liebermann agreed, and shortly afterward Anne-Marie was invited home to the Professor, who said she would like to consider her synopsis in more informal surroundings, as well as to talk with her about Denmark, since it was a country she was interested in. That is what she told Anne-Marie.

Anne-Marie put some things into a bag in her room in Hell's Kitchen and rode the subway across Manhattan to the address Gwen Liebermann had given her, and Anne-Marie, who as we know came from simple surroundings in provincial Denmark, did not realize until she arrived outside the Professor's home, that this was a fashionable place indeed. Professor Liebermann's was an exclusive residence on Madison Avenue, not far from Central Park, and the trees glistened with the spring as Anne-Marie arrived wearing sensible walking shoes and with her synopsis in her bag.

She went into the foyer and was greeted by a doorman in a bottle-green uniform. Before she could go anywhere else in the building, the doorman had to call up to the Professor, who vouched for her. She was shown into an elevator, and inside the elevator was another man in a bottle-green uniform. He was going to ride the elevator with her to the top floor, which, he said, on a good day commanded a splendid view. So it was that they ascended toward the heavens, and before they reached the top Anne-Marie had already thought to herself that living here could hardly be cheap.

The elevator door opened, the man in uniform extended his arm, and Anne-Marie stepped directly out into Professor Gwen Liebermann's apartment, which was not a regular apartment, but a penthouse. The Professor greeted her in a jacket and skirt and with a jangling string of pearls around her neck. As soon as they had shaken hands, Professor Liebermann gestured for Anne-Marie to sit down in a brown leather couch in front of a glass coffee table. The professor had mixed Martinis in small, smoke-colored glasses. Anne-Marie sat down and they raised their glasses with ice-cubes in them, while Gwen Liebermann thanked Anne-Marie for coming, and then they began to talk.

Anne-Marie had difficulty concentrating. The walls were hung with art, especially South American. The rooms were en suite, and the colors were heavy and earthy. The parquet flooring shone, and through the big windows you could see Madison Avenue down below and some of Central Park, where people were jogging with dogs on leashes. Being so taken by heights, Anne-Marie raised her gaze toward the eastern sky and thought about Silkeborg and how far she had come in such a short time in her life.

Anne-Marie felt comfortable sitting in these exclusive surroundings and listening to the Professor talk, even though she thought Liebermann was coming on unusually familiar with her. There was a change in Liebermann's character. Nothing pronounced, more like a slight dissonance in the way she was talking. It was like an opening up, an intimacy that was becoming all the more conspicuous, and then it happened.

"You're an ambitious girl, aren't you, Anne-Marie Jensen?" said the Professor, and Anne-Marie confirmed that this was so, and that she saw no reason not to work hard to achieve her goals.

"Is industry enough? Is talent or aptitude?" the Professor asked, and Anne-Marie, who sensed she was supposed to shake her head, shook her head.

"Is aptitude enough in a world governed by more primitive instincts, Anne-Marie?"

This was another loaded question, and Anne-Marie sat sipping her Martini as the Professor continued.

"What does a woman with a good head on her shoulders do in a world that basically couldn't care less about women who only have a good head on their shoulders?"

Anne-Marie shrugged, and Gwen Liebermann crossed her thin legs before asking Anne-Marie if she had had many lovers, and if she had one now, and Anne-Marie knew no better than to answer, and soon she found herself amid an avalanche of questions of a more or less directly sexual nature.

It transpired that Professor Gwen Liebermann really was interested in Denmark and in particular the famous Danish propensity for broad-mindedness, and Anne-Marie wondered for a while if the Professor might be lesbian, as one often suspects women like her of being. Yet her questions were not exclusively private and genital. More generally, she was interested in erotic relationships in the country from which Anne-Marie hailed. The motherland of free pornography. She had been told that Danish women lay topless on the ramparts of Copenhagen. She had heard that Danish men were not merely possessed by making a conquest of Danish women, but that they, too, would allow themselves to be won once in a while. This latter fact in particular was appreciated, Anne-Marie sensed from Gwen Liebermann's expression, and now Gwen Liebermann wanted to delve deeper into Anne-Marie's personal experiences of it.

"How do you like to make your conquests?" she asked, but Anne-Marie did not know what to say to that.

"There's no need to be shy, Anne-Marie," the Professor said. "I ask only because it's a matter of crucial importance if you wish to get on in life. Do you wish to get on in life, Anne-Marie?"

Anne-Marie sat there with her glass of Martini. She did not move until she found herself nodding, and then Liebermann clapped her hands together in triumph:

"Oh, la femme fatale! La femme fatale!"

That is what Liebermann said, and now she started talking about how she herself swore by her own inner femme fatale, because the inner femme fatale had its own remarkable will to possess the gaze of others, in particular of men, and thereby assume control of their existence in the world. A femme fatale could transform a man of power into a foolish boy who could be bridled by the gaze and by the threat (and the promise) of vaginal encounters.

"Coming from the homeland of Karen Blixen, I expect you know what I mean," Professor Liebermann went on. "The Baroness Blixen had control of her men. She was a conjuress of gender and identity, and look how well she got on. The Baroness Blixen, Anne-Marie—pay heed to the Baroness Blixen. Do you understand?"

Anne-Marie did not, but she smiled anyway.

"La femme fatale, indeed. On your way upward you must never forget la femme fatale, and you must never forget the story of Susanna at her Bath. Do you know the story of Susanna at her bath?"

Biblical stories were not Anne-Marie's strong point, but it didn't matter, because Professor Liebermann closed her eyes and said:

"Is anything more titillating for a woman who wishes to be seen and enjoyed, than the story of Susanna at her bath, naked and with her hair down and all the steam below? And the two elders watching and lusting after her. They watch, the two old men, as Susanna is enraptured by her own pleasure, seemingly unaware that she is beheld. Yet only seemingly so, because Susanna knows all about the eyes that behold. She is fully aware of the might she possesses. How she longs to have those old lechers in her power, Anne-Marie. How she loves the game whose center she commands. I am telling you this only that you might make your way in the world in which you wish to make your way. La femme fatale, Anne-Marie Jensen, la femme fatale."

Professor Liebermann, who as we know was dressed in a rather drab jacket and skirt, had now blushing cheeks as she raised her empty glass:

"New drinks!" she said, and went out into the kitchen to mix some.

Anne-Marie fumbled with her synopsis. The view of Madison Avenue and the rest of the world suddenly seemed dizzying and claustrophobic. It was not just that Gwen Liebermann appeared to be completely changed and was talking about things that made her feel insecure and shy. It was also the fact that Anne-Marie had always been so intent on doing the right thing through the right channels that she had never taken time to study the shadowy power structures of gender. To exploit her body so as to get on in the world was not a thing she had brought with her from home. In fact, she was wholly oblivious of topless girls on the ramparts of Copenhagen and of the desires of men to be won. She had had one boyfriend, Allan, through high school, and then a one-night stand in a tent at a music festival, and she now had a strong sense that this hardly made her an expert on sexual matters. And now she wanted to leave. But how to slip away from Gwen Liebermann's penthouse? Why this steamy interest in sex as an instrument of power? And how could Liebermann, on an ordinary professor's salary, afford to live in such opulence?

Anne-Marie felt piqued. Maybe even slightly angry about getting pinched between her synopsis, her nationality, and what clearly were the erotic fantasies of a middle-aged professor. But not only that: Amid the lecturing about woman's ability to control the masculine gaze by means of sex, thereby to achieve the goals one might set oneself without the brain getting in the way, Anne-Marie felt a strong urge to lift the lid on Professor Liebermann, maybe because the Professor seemed like she *wanted* her to lift the lid.

"This is a nice penthouse," Anne-Marie said when the Professor came back with new drinks.

"It is," said the Professor.

"It must be expensive?" said Anne-Marie.

"It is," said the Professor. "And how can that be, do you think, in this world in which a woman such as I never would be able to afford such a place? I mean, we are art historians, Anne-Marie. We are experts in ways of seeing. And appearances, my dear, are everything. Am I right? So how do you think I can afford all this?"

There was no anger in Liebermann's voice, and Anne-Marie said it like it was: She didn't know.

The Professor leaned back in the leather couch and again raised the subject of Anne-Marie's homeland.

"You're Danish," she said. "Considering where you come from, I don't suppose it matters. Besides, as I'm sure you've noticed, you're alone, *entirely* alone in my apartment. But you must keep quiet. Do you promise? Because if you promise, I shall tell you my secret."

Anne-Marie glanced out of the panorama window and promised to keep quiet.

"I have a little sideline," the Professor said. "And my little sideline is to be kept a secret. Now I shall explain."

It turned out that the secrecy in the main was necessary because Gwen Liebermann, as her name suggested, was of Jewish descent and moreover was involved in raising considerable funds in the affluent conservative circles of Manhattan's Jewish community. The money she raised went directly into the coffers of the big, modern museum. Gwen Liebermann, then, was a woman compelled, whenever circumstance deemed it appropriate, to lead a life of propriety subject to what from the outside appeared to be a strict sense of moral values. And it was no easy matter to lead a double life.

Professor Liebermann got to her feet, went over to the bookcase and picked out a number of volumes. She carried them almost ceremoniously over to Anne-Marie and placed them on the table between their smoke-colored Martini glasses.

"Look closely at these books," Liebermann said.

Anne-Marie pulled the nearest one toward her and could see it was written by one Betsy Bartlett and that it was about sex. A quick glance at the others was enough to tell her that they were all written by Betsy Bartlett and that they all were about sex. Gwen Liebermann appeared to be excited, and her excitement made the whole room thrum. She leaned forward, opened a book, found the photo on the jacket flap and turned it toward Anne-Marie.

The jacket photo showed a youngish woman. She was red-haired, and she looked like something in Kodachrome from 1955: the dress, the make-up, the heavy sensuality of her gaze—a true temptress with that particular combination of sex, delectability and power that can make men, regardless of age, act like small boys given a dollar for candy.

"This woman," Professor Liebermann said, pointing with a dry finger, "is Betsy Bartlett. One of the most highly paid authors of erotic literature in the United States. And this woman—Betsy Bartlett—is me."

Anne-Marie saw Professor Liebermann straighten up, swaying slightly, thrusting her hips forward beneath her skirt, and she looked down at the jacket photo of the red-haired demi-monde, Betsy Bartlett, smiling beneath a pair of hypnotic eyes that quite clearly belonged to Professor Liebermann.

Anne-Marie had once collected ladybugs in matchboxes on the banks of the lake as she sang *Ladybug, ladybug fly away home*, but now she thought it seemed so long ago, and her eyes flickered feverishly from Betsy to Gwen, from Gwen to Betsy. Yet she said nothing, and that was something either Gwen Liebermann or Betsy Bartlett did not care for, so whoever it was pushed the books closer to Anne-Marie and said:

"Well, go on, look at them!"

Anne-Marie did as she was told. She looked at the images of the writer of erotic books. There was one of her standing above a subway grate with her skirt up to her ears. There was another in which she was made up to look like Modesty Blaise. There was one of her in patent leather boots with stiletto heels, with a glistening python wrapped around her. Another showed her lying in front of the palace at Versailles, her red hair tangled in the grass, orgastic, dreamy and rapt, with a joint in her hand.

"It's a wig," Professor Liebermann explained as she sat down and took a long, slender cigarillo from a box on the table. "It's a red wig and the make-up is camouflage. I wear a corset so as to change my figure, and Betsy Bartlett always wears the kind of jewelry a professor wouldn't. My clothes are carefully selected to entice the beholder away from the fact that to begin with I was just a person who had worked hard and studied for a long time. You would be surprised how easy it is, Anne-Marie Jensen. I turn myself into a vamp in the bathroom, and it's been going on for years."

Professor Gwen Liebermann crossed her legs in a new, leggy kind of way. No-one had ever suspected, she said. No-one had ever believed that the two women were one and the same person. Only once had it almost gone wrong, and that was the time Betsy Bartlett was invited to go on a talkshow on primetime television:

"My boss at the museum had turned on the TV and seen a youngish woman in a floral-patterned dress and nice shoes talking about how best to handle the male member. While the red-haired woman, who was me, was describing how to masturbate a man, the camera zoomed in on my hands. My boss recognized my hands as they wrapped around this banana that was supposed to be a penis, and the next day he took me aside and asked me always to wear gloves whenever I was on TV. It was a very serious matter, he said, and all the while he looked me up and down. He said that if I wasn't careful in the future, it might jeopardize donations. He said he was highly attracted to me and didn't know what to do about it. I said *comme çi, comme ça*, and since then everything in the museum world has been smooth as silk. Do you understand what I'm saying, Anne-Marie?"

Anne-Marie saw the Professor's index finger tap the ash from her cigarillo.

"I put on gloves. That's what I do," she said. It's very simple. What do you need your talents for, Anne-Marie, if the world's just going to crap on them?"

Gwen Liebermann clattered her ice-cubes against her glass. She sniggered, and Anne-Marie from Silkeborg sniggered, too, and felt like her hands were all sticky. Anne-Marie sniggered, but not for the same reason. The Professor sniggered because she was two people who could pull the wool over people's eyes and thereby get on a lot quicker in the world. But the girl from Denmark sniggered because she was dangling in the air with no idea of how to get down and find herself and find her way home again. She sniggered because all of a sudden she was having difficulty recognizing herself, the youngest child of her parents, in this scenario. She sniggered because she was ashamed of once having had sex with a Swede in a tent. She sniggered because she was terrified by the thought that the Professor was an empty frame in which Betsy Bartlett could hide away and step out and make things happen whenever it was appropriate.

"If you don't think blowjobs can pave your way in the big, modern museum, you're more naïve than you look, Anne-Marie Jensen. Do you want to get on in the world?"

"I don't know," said Anne-Marie, even though it was the wrong thing to say.

"Do you want to get on, and can you see what I'm saying?" the Professor repeated.

Anne-Marie nodded and downed the contents of her glass, ice-cubes and all.

"If you can see what I'm saying, then I'll show you in practice."

Anne-Marie tried to put her synopsis back into her bag.

"Do you want to see?"

Anne-Marie did not nod, or maybe she did anyway. It was hard to say. Everything went so fast, almost by reflex. And the next thing was the Professor got to her feet, her joints snapping, and went out to the bathroom.

The battle that went on inside the young woman from Denmark while Professor Liebermann turned from professor to demi-monde is hard to describe. She was willing and unwilling all at once. She really didn't want to, and yet she sat immovably with a view of it all. Indeed, she felt compelled to remain seated: Professor Liebermann did not seem to be the kind of person anyone would want to have against them at the university or at the big, modern museum, and Anne-Marie Jensen spent most of these few moments glancing toward the elevator door. She hoped the elevator door would open, that it would slide to one side and that the bottle-green man would be standing there looking like a kind father without the slightest sexual interest in her at all. He would say that she was a good girl and that she had to come with him now. That was what he should say—that he was going to take her down again and that he would show her the right way home. But it was not the elevator door that opened. When finally something opened, it was the bathroom door. The bathroom door opened and a person stepped out.

"Well, here I am," said Betsy Bartlett, pulling on her glove. And from there on in, there was no turning back.

Translated from the Danish by Martin Aitken

NINE LIVES OF THE COUGAR

Duff Brenna

One

It is 1999, a Friday and there is no way she can know that leaving Lariat's with him is a mistake, one that will determine her future.

Thrilling though, hugging his back, cheek on his shoulder, her red hair flaming behind her, the roar of the engine throbbing like a direct link to the core of everything primitive.

Ah, this is living!

LARGE—the way she always wants it. Forty-four years to his what? Twenty-one, twenty-two? She's guessing. But whatever his age, she's not exactly robbing the cradle. Is she?

The sexual tension had been palpable the instant he asked her if he could sit down, buy her a drink. Long lanky luscious Italian. Or maybe Spanish?

Eye embers glittering behind lids slit thin as paper when he smiled at her.

"Sure, why not?" she told him. She liked his leather vest. She liked his silver-toed boots. She liked his wavy hair.

"Mike Cavuto," he said, leaning towards her, shaking her hand. "And you're Colleen."

She raised her eyebrows.

He nodded towards the bar, towards Arthur mixing a martini. "I asked him. He said you always come in on Fridays."

"The music. The dancing. You like dancing?"

He shrugged his shoulders. "Not much of a dancer," he said. "Slow ones are okay."

A remark that made her lose interest in him. Until her fifth margarita.

It's 1999, a Friday. The sky is bright with stars crowding each other as the Harley flies from Hemet chasing a moonless countryside. Cows at pasture lumpish as black boulders haphazardly scattered. Black trees fanning behind them. A farm house in the distance, a light on the second floor like a beacon. Someone in bed reading? It's 1999 and not yet midnight. The motorcycle weaving from one curve to another. Hills go up. Hills go down. The headlamp searching whatever is waiting for them.

Colleen is frightened, thrillingly frightened. She loves scary motorcycles. She's been in love with danger since her husband died and freed her. She doesn't really believe anything bad will happen. The way Mike handles the Harley is masterful. She thinks about taking him home. She thinks about her two children, her twelve-year-old son, her fifteen-year-old daughter in their beds sleeping, the TV on for company. She had locked the house down and left her kids oblivious. The drone of television masking her absence. She knows if they wake, it won't be a problem. She's trained them. They're used to Friday nights without the mommy. If she brings Mike home, the children know not to fuss or be a bother. She'll have him gone before breakfast tomorrow.

She is on the verge of leaning forward, her mouth to Mike's ear telling him to turn around and take her back to her car, follow her home. If he wants to. What if he doesn't want to?

Don't be silly, he wants to. All men want to. Even at forty-four no one has ever turned her down, not even married men. It's fun, but she doesn't do it too often. Once a month if the mood strikes her.

"Mike," she says, "let's go back, it's late. You can—"

The headlight spears an Angus big as a boulder blocking the road. Mike leans hard, the pavement a few inches from her knee before the bike straightens and rockets into and through a row of rural mailboxes. Colleen flying. She is upside down and where did Mike go? Colleen has no time to look for him, her head and arms hit gravel, the rest of her crumbling, tumbling, bones breaking, liver bursting. All of her instantly painless. No thoughts. Nothing.

Two

It's 1999, Friday night. Colleen's legs are weary from so much dancing with this slow swinger named Mike Cavuto. Pleasantly tired, her brain pleasantly buzzing. Mike asks if she wants a quick spin on his Harley. He is pressing her against the car. His hands caressing her hips tugging. She feels his tumescence. It's almost midnight and she knows lovemaking would be the right ending to such a raw night. Lovemaking to soothe her, all wound up as she is from dancing drinking flirting. Fondling legs moving across the floor.

She's sure this boy dry-humping her is close to two decades younger, twenty-one, twenty-two. Too young for her forty-four years, but she can handle him. She handles all of them fine, all the men she handles them.

"Follow me, come home with me," she whispers, breathing the words into his ear as he nuzzles her neck and presses harder into her.

Caressing her hair, he smells it and says, "I heard a rumor redheads are wild in bed."

"Follow me. It's just around the corner, not far," she tells him, words that will determine her future.

He hesitates. He's staring at his hands in her hair and hesitating. "Sexy hair," he murmurs. "I like it long like this. Pixie hair is a turn off."

"Are you married?" she asks him.

"Never fear," he tells her. "Lead the way, babe."

She doesn't like the word *babe*, but for now she doesn't say anything.

At home, while Mike goes to the bathroom, she checks on the kids and notes how sweet they look sleeping, cheeks flushed, mouths gaping. Cathy's hair spread over the pillow, a red streak caught in the gleam, a glimmer of light from the open door. The rest of her hair seems dyed auburn fading to black in the shadows. Liam Junior is still a towhead. His thin, pale arms lie outside the covers, pale hands folding over his chest, fingers layered. He reminds her of his father, the way his father used to sleep, layered hands guarding his stomach. The same way he looked in his coffin.

Mike comes up behind her. Puts a hand on her shoulder.

Whispering she tells him, "Cathy and Liam Junior."

"Beauties," says Mike. "How old are they?"

She gives him their ages as she leads him away to the bedroom, the bed.

Three

The lovemaking is as good as she thought it would be. Nothing like a young-younger man who can stay the course several times over with very little prompting. Liam had been like that when they first got together, just teenagers wrestling in the backseat of his parents' Buick. It was 1971, the two of them exploring the mystery. The two of them hot-blooded, full of sap.

And then he joined the Army. By 1972 he was playing war. She waited for him. She waited faithfully. In 1973 he was discharged with a medical—something wrong with his lungs. The effect of Agent Orange. He learned to function as a bookkeeper at the Ford dealership. But he never got over the exfoliate kicked up in the dust by his boots, sprinkling down his neck from dying vegetation above him, breathed in with every breath. He functioned as a man battling numerous ailments, a surfeit that aged him. Always tired. Always cranky.

Dead two years now. Died of leukemia. Army saying not its fault, not this late in the game. It was 1997 when she buried him. Six months later she went to Lariat's. And scored. Easily.

She wakes with the sun, but Mike is already gone. She has no idea what time he left. Maybe he's one of those guys who don't like to stay all night. Fearing, perhaps, that waking in the morning cuddling a woman puts her on the inside, giving her a claim on him. Or maybe he just had to go to work early and was being polite, tip-toeing around so he wouldn't wake her. If it were that she'd be fine, no problem. Mike, come and go as you please. Where does he work? Didn't he say something about construction? A carpenter, maybe?

He did tell her he would meet her at Lariat's Friday, didn't he?

Four

It's 1999, Friday night and Colleen has her table, the one Arthur set aside for her between the bar, the barstools, and the curving edge of the dance floor, narrow pillars to the right and left of her, more tables leading to the side wall and the front wall behind her. The band is playing, warming up with Deana Carter's "Did I Shave my Legs for This?" Colleen sips beer and hums along. The clock says 9:50. The place is lively. Couples chatting laughing at the tables. Friends crowding the booths. Every barstool full. Waitresses scurrying. Arthur and Jason filling orders.

Colleen feels happy sitting in the midst of it all. She keeps glancing towards the door. Lots of people tumbling in arm and arm, or alone, or holding hands, or following each other searching for places to sit. She recognizes some of them. For a moment she thinks one of the men is Mike Cavuto. But nope.

Soon the dancing starts again. The floor is jumping. The music titillating. She closes her eyes and listens to hard country—fiddles, guitars, drums, piano. It takes a moment to recognize the voice: Wade Hayes: "Old Enough to Know Better." She closes her eyes. She daydreams.

This night she has arranged to have the whole house to herself. She's left the kids with her parents. She's bought a case of Budweiser. She's bought chips and three kinds of dip.

She'll coax him to take her home early. She'll make him comfy on the couch. Put on a CD. Something sexy to wire him, set a wild mood before changing to slow romantic: Carter's "Strawberry Wine." They'll dance to that, sweet swaying, no need to move much, just rhythmically letting his hands work, letting their lips touch. Gluey lips, slippery tongues. The vision of it rises like copulating phantoms inside her head. Young stuff. Fresh, not all used up.

"Care to dance, pretty lady?"

She opens her eyes. No, it's not Mike. Some teenaged cowpoke with a beer-drinker's belly ten weeks pregnant. But nice looking otherwise, firm beardless jaw, clear eyes youthful blue. Are they blue? Hard to tell in the dimmed lights.

"Oh, I'm sorry," she says. "I'm waiting for someone."

The man looks around. Says, "If you was my gal, I'd never leave you sittin alone in a joint like this."

"He got held up," she says, hoping he'll not try to engage her, hoping he'll take the hint and leave. He tips his Stetson and tries his luck elsewhere. It isn't long before she sees him with a woman whose jeans are so tight across her ass the seams are separating. He has his hands on her hips. She has her hands around his neck. Actually, he's a very graceful dancer, carrying his belly as if it isn't there.

The door keeps opening. More people arriving. Some people leaving. She looks at the halo clock hanging high over the register. Where did the time go? Thirty minutes after eleven. But surely he'll come. He will come. Won't he? She doesn't recall if they set a time.

It was: Friday night.

It was: I'll be there.

It was: I'll be there if you will, babe.

Time riding the earth and the band plays on. The couples move fervidly. All of them sweat-drenched. All of them feverish.

Somehow the men know not to ask her to dance. She sits isolated, feeling like a leper. She switches from beer to bourbon with waterback.

Almost before she knows it, there are five glasses of water crowding her table. Five shot glasses and she's drunk. She didn't mean to get drunk. She wonders if she can walk. She wonders if she can drive her car.

It's after midnight before she tries to move. Nope no way.

Plop goes her fanny.

Another shot of amber appears. She looks up at the waitress who says, "Arthur on the house."

It's Arthur who gets her home after he locks up. It's Arthur, big-shouldered and bald who ends up in bed with her.

He rises at noon. He showers and dresses, kisses her on the lips and says, "Whoa, babe, you got dragon breath."

"My head," she says, rolling over.

He chuckles. She feels him patting her butt. She hears the door open and close. "Water," she cries out. But he's already gone.

Five

It's 1971, an easy summer after basic training and Liam can't seem to get enough of her. Five times already and the other couple knocking on the motel door asking if they want to go eat. "Later," Liam hollers. "Nymphos," says the muffled voice of his boot camp buddy Trenton. Liam goes back to working on her. Kissing her, licking her, half his fist inside her while he says how much he missed her, how much he thought about her every night and couldn't keep from kissing his pillow. Couldn't keep from masturbating.

"All those guys in the shower, all those butts, some of em very fine, very feminine, so feminine you even start thinking about them. At our age, once you've had it you can't get over it."

She can't talk. She listens to him. She's all sexed-up, the core of her radiating heat to the tips of her ears the tips of her toes. They've been fucking so long and hard she's getting sore, but she doesn't want to stop anymore than Liam does. He keeps whispering, "God, I wanted you so badly, Colleen I went a little crazy, I think. Boot camp was like being in stir."

It was an amazing time and then he had to go back to camp and they didn't see each other until after he came home from the war.

Six

It is 1972. Liam no longer a horny boy. A man with jittery hands now. A man with night sweats and bad dreams and impotence. He tells her he should have never gone into the Army. He says one wrong move ruined his life. He says there is no going back to correct the mistakes we make. Determinism, not God, rules everyone, he says. Once you go off-course, you're off-course forever, he says.

It takes him nine months and three shots of vodka and a lot of oral sex before he finally gets it up enough to fuck her. She hopes with a little help they can duplicate the day and night in the motel a year ago. But he is only good for one round before he falls asleep, his damp head on her breasts. His heavy breathing turning into childish whimpering that makes her feel repulsion. She wants to help him. She wants to be the courageous woman who stays by his side. She wants to be a heroine.

Seven

And she is. She stays with him. They marry with much fanfare in 1973. Many barren years go by, until at last in 1983, she is pregnant with Cathy. Liam on Ativan by then, enough to get him through the day. Ativan is thought to be the reason he coughs so much when he wakes in the morning.

Three years later she is pregnant again. They are trying for a boy. They are trying for Liam Jr.

Junior grows up nervous-tetchy like his father. Always anxious about school. Picked on. Beaten up. Unable to obey his father's command to fight back. Every black eye, bloody nose, split lip his father takes personally. His father takes the boy by the hair and shakes him back and forth and yells. "No son of mine is a coward! I'm a war vet, dammit!"

"Tomorrow you go up to that bully and punch him in the nose!"

"When you see him, go after him, Junior! Knock his teeth down his throat!"

"Junior, a coward dies a thousand deaths, the brave dies but one!"

"Kick him in the balls, Junior!"

"Take a bat and bash his head in, Junior!"

"Why can't you be a warrior like your old man? Kick some ass!"

Junior never kicks ass. He hides out behind the bleachers in the gym. He hides out in the bathroom in the stalls, his feet on the toilet seat, his eyes now and then above the rim of the door spying, worrying about his enemies finding him.

By the time he is ten and his father dies, Liam Jr. is a wreck who is flunking everything and needs not only tranquillizers but therapy. He is diagnosed with attention deficit and given lithium. He is put on Medi-Cal and sent to a school for autistics and retards.

Eight

It's 1999, a Friday night at Lariat's. Colleen O'Leary is sitting at her favorite table waiting for Mike Cavuto and listening to country music. She is watching the dancers. She sips a slow-gin fizz, sweet enough to make her tongue restless. She closes her eyes. She dreams of a week ago Friday. "Let me take you for a ride, babe." If he comes tonight, she'll let him rocket her into the stars.

"Care to dance, pretty lady?"

She opens her eyes. No, it's not Mike. Some teenaged cowpoke with a beer-drinker's belly ten weeks pregnant. But nice looking otherwise, firm beardless jaw, clear eyes youthful blue. Are they blue? Hard to tell in the dimmed lights. She darts a look over her shoulder. She looks at the door. She looks at the clock. He ain't coming, she tells herself.

"Sure, why not?" she says.

Possessively he supports the small of her back as he moves her to the floor. He spins her. He grasps her hips. She puts her hands on his shoulders. They dance and she likes his dancing. Pot belly or no he's fluid.

"How old are you?" she says.

"Old enough," he says.

"Barely legal, I'd say."

"My name's Bodie Ray," he drawls, smiling. His teeth looking like baby teeth.

"Colleen O'Leary," she says.

"Irish."

"Mostly."

They dance. They drink. She wonders why he wasn't carded. "Eighteen?" she says. "Nineteen?"

"Does it matter?"

She considers his question. She shakes her head. She says, "Except you could be my son, Bodie."

"Now that's a thought," he says. "You got a son?"

She tells him about Liam Junior and Cathy.

Bodie orders another round. "Chugalug," he says.

Time measures their conversation, their coordination. *Blue ain't the word*...twangs the guitar man.

The door opens and Mike strolls in, same jeans, same leather vest, same silver-toed cowboy boots. He spots her, comes over, says, "Bike broke down, babe. Sorry." Looking at his greasy hands he says. "I gotta wash up."

While Mike is washing up, Bodie asks, "Is that the cowboy you waitin on?"

"I was."

"Past tense?"

She tries to think it over, but her mind is cloudy. Her mind is boozed. "I feel foggy," she says.

"C'mon," he says and leads her back to the dance floor.

Over his shoulder she sees Mike regarding her. Her impulse is to go to him. Her impulse is to say, "Excuse me, Bodie," and go to Mike's arms. But before she can do that, he turns on his heel. He leaves Lariat's.

A moment later she hears the Harley wrapping–Wrap! Wrap!–as if it's saying: Get your ass out here!

Long after midnight Bodie escorts her to her car, says he was dropped off, asks her for a ride. They end up at her house. She looking in on the kids with him standing beside her, his hand on her ass, kneading it. She says to herself, she says, Colleen O'Leary, you are sooo easy, girl.

The sex is quick. The sex is over in a minute, maybe two, with Colleen hardly feeling anything. Did she? Did she not? He keeps kissing her, touching her, trying to light her fire again, but she is fading. The last thing she feels is Bodie against her hip. Him getting hard again.

"Not now, Mike," she says. "Morning."

"Mike?" says Bodie. "I'm Bodie Ray, not fuckin Mike."

"Rain check," she says. "Catch you in the morning."

She passes out. Vaguely dreamily she feels rubbing, she feels probing. Soon she feels...

Nothing.

Until she wakes hearing someone screaming, shouting. It's Cathy's voice, some man's voice saying "Oh baby oh baby." On crumbling feet,

Colleen careers down the hall into walls into the bedroom, where she sees her daughter naked and him naked on top of her pumping away, his ass rising and falling. Junior comes in the door holding a kitchen knife, flashing by her, stabbing the man named Bodie, stabbing him twice. Colleen snatches the knife from his hand. Bodie rises. He turns on her, trying to take the knife away. She slashes his hands. He stumbles out of the room, stumbling over the floor, stumbling out the front door. Where he starts yelling, "Help! Help! Murder! Help!" Naked man (bare ass, pot belly and all) fumbling toward the road. His cries weakening. His legs caving under him. Rises once to his knees. Falls onto his side heavily, a thump like raw dough hitting a breadboard.

Nine

It is 1999. Junior's mother brings a man home whose name is Mike Cavuto. Junior has seen a lot of men come and go, but Mike isn't one of them. At least not yet. He is a lot younger than Junior's mother, but in some ways he seems older, seems like a man in charge. He is a carpenter. He is mechanical. He can do electrical work. He can fix the plumbing. Over the course of several weeks, he and Junior work together getting the house in apple-pie order.

One night Junior hears his mother and Mike talking in the kitchen. They are sitting at the table and she says, "No, Mike, it wouldn't work. I'm too old for you. There's nearly twenty years between us, honey."

"As if that means anything," he says. "Age is only a number. I've been looking for you all my life, Colleen. And I'm thinking you been looking for me too."

Junior hears his mother sobbing softly. He hears her say, "Oh Mike, oh Mike, if only it could be. Why didn't you come along years ago?"

"It's not only if it could be, babe, it is! I love you. I love your kids. That boy of yours, he's crazy about me. He doesn't say much, but he's always hanging around. He wants to watch what I'm doing. He wants to hand me tools. I taught him how to adjust the valves on the Harley today. I tell you if I get time with that kid, he'll make liars out of everyone who says he's retarded, those who call him autistic. That's bullshit, babe. There's nothing wrong with that kid except the world won't give him a break."

"Cathy won't like it, Mike. Cathy resents you already. She says you're more her age than mine."

"Ah Cathy, don't sweat her, Colleen. She's just a mental case like all teens are for a while. I was, wasn't you? She'll come around. I'll charm her, you'll see. Too bad she doesn't like motorcycles. I told her I'd teach her to ride, but she said no way, Jay." Junior hears him laughing. Whenever Mike laughs, Junior's heart swells so much he fears it might burst.

There is a long pause and then Mike says, "Look at it this way, babe. She's gonna grow up and find someone and leave you. And so will Liam Junior. Ten, maybe twelve years down the road, they'll be out of here and only me and you then, only each other. What we do now will determine what comes after, so you gotta think careful. This will determine your future, babe. This will determine our future. Okay, we don't have to get married. I don't care that much about it. But let's just say it's like we're married. We'll be faithful. We'll be long-time commitment lovers. Only problem I can see is your folks. Since I ain't got none, it's all about you, babe. You'd have to persuade them. I think they like me a little, don't you?"

"Well enough," she says. "Mom called me Cougar the other day. I think she's a little jealous. Dad...I don't know what Dad thinks. He never says much. Mom always ruled the house. Yeah, well, she did ask me if I thought you'd stick around. I said it seemed like you wanted to, but I learned with my husband not to count on anyone being the same everyday for the rest of their lives. Something happens and people change. The difference between the old Liam and the postwar Liam was black and white, night and day. But I wanted to be the noble woman. I wanted to sacrifice myself for a good cause."

"You got Liam Junior and Cathy out of it," says Mike.

They quit talking. Junior peeks around the corner. Mike is leaning across the table kissing her, his hand cupping her breast.

Junior knows something instantly. Instantly he sees what his mother sees in Mike. A good man. Dependable. Thoughtful. Good with his hands. No doubt a great kisser as well. Quivers of love run through the boy's body. He understands how important her decision is. He understands that her decision will make or break him. He understands the next moment will determine his future.

WHAT WE WANT

Laura McCullough

The mortician knows his job,   makes his money:
    we all want to look lovely when we go,
    or at least used up,
    like we took the ride as far as it would go,
        got out, and jumped.

This poem in my belly makes me nauseas
    as chemicals hit
    the chemicals we are—
    which ones will kill, which ones save?

It's all an empty sky, but your hair looks better
    than it did when you were alive,
    and someone whispers,
    do you think she just had good bones, to look so good?
Thin threads holding it all together—
    we whisperers in the corner, praisers
        of the makeup, sewn lips and lids.
I wish he'd do me, someone else says,
    snickers from the teenager
    who doesn't get any of this
    and doesn't understand she can wear her hair
        any which way,

dress in paper bags,
            and her age would make her radiant.

We close in around her, oh, we know it   we want it
    we touch her red hair,
    take the strand she is sucking on from her lips.
    Your time will come, we smile;
    we smile in the empty air
    we shape into poems
    reclaiming fear,
        meanness much easier to stand

and our eyes turning red   red   red
    reveal everything we wish
        we could say, but can not.

BEAUTY SALON LOVE

Laura McCullough

He says, Oh, I understand your hair, you need...
    and rattles off a litany that includes
        coconut oil infusion
    after, of course, a clarifying shampoo,
        and talks curl shape and cuticle health
    and color, oh, we'll talk color next time;
            your red is so good, we don't need to go there yet,
                but when we do, you're in the right hands,

and I admit, I started to weep,
    not a lot, but yes, the kind like when you've finally made love
    rather than had sex
    and the whole sweep of your future
    suddenly opens both out to that future
    and back to the dream
    you had as a little girl of being rescued
    and loved
    for ever and ever and ever
and suddenly I could make love to my new hair-guy,
    but instead buy close to two hundred dollars worth of products,
    everything he says will transform me,
    and I nod as he takes my money,
        and would kiss him if he let me,

and then I go home to my husband,
    and tell him, I like the new salon,
        but in our bedroom I hide the bag
        with the shampoo, curl activator, and everything else
        I will rub in my palms,
        apply to my head, every day until I can go back,
        spend a little more,

hoping the husband won't find it,
    knowing he will,
        knowing he'll forgive me my desperation,
        this lapse in judgment,

and he'll say, you always look beautiful to me,
    and I'll smile with gratitude,
        and won't tell him
            how that's just not enough.

COLLECTOR

Line-Maria Lång

There is a sea by a river where only female plants grow. The girl comes there often. She laughs with the plants and doesn't care that it's raining. The mosquitoes swarm around her and settle on her bare white arms and cover her ankles and throat. She waves goodbye to them when they've drunk their greedy full and float away in the wind like tiny red balloons that are smashed against the earth.

She has heard that there are rare fish in the water, and that is why she walks out there so carefully. People usually throw coins and messages in bottles into the water. Those she finds the girl gathers in her dress. She feels her way forward, breaking through the thick air with her every movement. Leaves fall from the trees and land before her in the water: even if the contact is only brief, they create a rustling wall of sound, everything contributes to a great surface, a gigantic instrument, a combined will to make noise. The fish are amused; they dart and swim between her feet. They open their toothless mouths and suckle her toes with gentle bites. She floats, and the fish are like ten white horses working beneath her; she strokes them and blows smoke on them. She doesn't know whether they've had her completely underwater to greet her, but something inside her, the smoke and the air, draws her ribcage up, when it is filled, like the messages in bottles that sink and bob up. They want to be found.

She rolls laughing toward the bank, but begins to wonder whether she can open her eyes again, whether they are already open now. When she dozes, she thinks about whether she will wake, but it doesn't matter, she is so happy just as she is.

So much sky. So much sky. So much sky. The grass prickles and lifts her from the earth, she hangs on each blade like someone running over needles. So much blue in the world, she thinks.

Nearby a man sweeps the stairs and collects refuse; he is working so early that for others it is still night. He gathers things that should not have been discarded, and that night he has already found a small paper ship made of red tissue paper, a bottle with a message in it which he looks forward to reading, and a flat chanterelle. The lamellas had all with a single footstep been pressed into one another so they formed a picture on the ground. When he was a child he only collected flat things, felt that a special unity occurred, that the flattening turned it into a snapshot. All the flat earthworms that crawled somewhere, a flat ladybug with its red outer wings spread to the side like a gown for an old-fashioned ball with a little train of the actual wings, black and transparent, trailing after it. He found flat sparrows and let them float in the water. A flat plastic mug that could be taken up cleanly with a cookie spatula. There had to be a flat person who could drink from it. A flat person who walked around smoking a flat cigarette and lived in a flat house and slid in and out of the front door like a letter.

He collects the garbage in large bags with four strings that must be tied first the one way, then the other. He always walks through a park to empty the refuse cans, and it is often the same as in the garbage bags, cracked plastic wine glasses, dead wasps in white napkins, sandwich halves, the man is so interested.

He sees the girl on the bank; she lays there, her eyes closed. He thinks that she is some kind of sculpture of hard plaster, a mannequin that hasn't been put in a bag and bound with knots or bows. He thinks she is a thing he can take home and save. That is what he does. He puts her in the most beautiful bag he's found, one he has been saving. He ties a fine double bow, and he is a little sorry that her legs have been made that way, with red, swollen marks and the neck, which is covered with small bumps, and the completely transparent toe nails that are so clean, it doesn't look natural. He carries her home, and she is heavier than he would have thought. He sets her in a room where he keeps special things. There he saves her, and as the first of her type in his collection, she will be something completely special.

Translated from the Danish by Thomas E. Kennedy

CAYENNE PEPPER

Steve Heller

Sheyene Foster Lager. Shy and Lost Her Feller. The Kid. The Old Lady. Woody Woodpecker. One Non-Blonde. Cayenne Pepper.

These are all names I have used to refer to my wife, Sheyene Foster Heller, who is nearly three decades my junior. At 19, Sheyene (pronounced like the town in Wyoming) was the red-haired girl who wrenched my life from its established course and gave it a new one. We've been married for a decade now. Along the way, the Heller family has been reconstructed: conflicts settled, wounds healed, new loving relationships forged and tempered. Perhaps not surprisingly, Sheyene's hair is no longer red but honey blond, bleached by sun and years. What follows is not a story of lives changed and a family reconfigured but rather a kaleidoscopic view of the enduring personalities of the woman who has given me a second life.

Sheyene Foster Lager is a pun that dates back to our early years together—though, even then, her drink of choice was usually bourbon, preferably the faux bourbon called Jack Daniels. The first time the subject came up, she was too young to consume alcohol legally.

"Just water for me," she said when the waitress in the green restaurant in Portland asked what we'd like to drink.

"Mind if I have a scotch?"

"No, please go right ahead."

I could tell from the tone of her affirmation she wished she could order one too.

"Johnny Walker Red, neat."

When the waitress left, Sheyene asked: "That means without ice, right?"

"Exactly... Do you drink?"

"Oh, yes...whenever I don't have to produce an ID."

"And where would that be?"

"Oh, Auntie Mae's or The Gin Mill, for example. They both have back doors where your friends can let you in."

"Ah, teamwork."

When the waitress set down my scotch, I told her we'd need a few more minutes. When my eyes returned to Sheyene, she was staring at my glass.

"You don't want any water with that?"

"A water back is always good, but we already have water on the table."

Her face turned a shade of pink I'd never seen before.

The conversation was beginning to make me feel oddly parental, as if I were talking with my oldest son David about how Dad learned to drink responsibly. I took a sip of the Red and asked: "So what do you drink when the backdoor's unlocked?"

"Oh...beer. Or Jack and Coke."

I must have raised my eyebrows at the latter, because I could read the mental note forming just behind her frontal lobes: No Coke.

Later on, in her legal years, I would watch Sheyene Foster Lager learn to drink Jack Daniels neat, then quickly give up bourbon altogether because it was "too sweet." By then she was reading Dorothy Parker and Lillian Hellman, and scotch had become her drink too. *These women are my role models*, she'd tell me, and read me a Parker poem or a passage from Hellman's *Pentimento*.

"Good writers, sad women," I observed one day.

"No, they're *funny*! Listen to this," she said, opening her *Portable Dorothy Parker*. She reads me "The Leal," the comic poem that concludes: "The while I know that every foe/Is faithful till I die."

"I dare you to tell me that isn't funny."

"You know, you're awfully young to adopt cynicism as your world view."

"Really? What age cynic would marry a middle-aged gas bag with four children?"

One who's too young to know the difference, I might have replied, but by this point Sheyene Foster Lager already knew plenty.

We rented movies from the 30's with Katherine Hepburn, Rosalind Russell, Barbara Stanwick, Irene Dunn, and Myrna Loy. *Those were the days*, Sheyene would say. *Those are my kind of gals: Tough. Smart. Independent.* We were watching one of *The Thin Man* movies one evening, and I noticed Sheyene staring wistfully at the screen as Nick and Nora sipped clear-colored liquid from funnel-shaped glasses and bantered with each other in a bar. At the end of the scene, Sheyene asked me what went into a martini.

"A classic martini is made with gin and a whisper of vermouth," I replied. "And at least one olive."

She made a sour face. "I don't like gin."

"What kind have you had?"

"I don't know...Gordon's?"

"No wonder. It doesn't matter what you put in a gin and tonic, but a martini requires top-drawer gin."

"Mmmmm..." She shook her head. "What about vodka?"

"I actually started out drinking vodka martinis with my colleague Rob. But a vodka martini isn't a real martini. It's an imposter."

Sheyene pushed the pause button on the VCR and leaned against me. "Would you make me an imposter martini?"

I reached into the freezer and pulled out a clear bottle. "Fortunately, we have Stoli."

It didn't take long before the martini was our drink of choice, at Harry's Uptown or at home. At Harry's I would order mine as a Gibson, with a pearl onion instead of an olive, so the waitress wouldn't get confused about who got which glass. At home I taught Sheyene Foster Lager to shake rather than stir, and to prefer queen or king-size olives. Gin, however, was another matter.

Then one night we ran out of Stoli. Sheyene watched enviously as I got out a martini glass for me, and a smaller cocktail glass for her scotch. "What kind of gin is that?" she asked.

"Bombay Sapphire...the best."

She crinkled her nose, then shrugged. "What the hell. I'll try one."

Once you go blue, nothing else tastes true. Even though, as my Antioch colleague Al Erdynast will attest, Sheyene and I do love a good single malt whenever we can get it, any bartender who recognized us in our Kansas days would automatically start mixing a Bombay Sapphire martini, straight-up, with olives and a whisper of vermouth.

"You're getting too good at this," I warned her one evening when she asked me to make her another. We were listening to John Coltrane while we graded papers.

"What do you mean?"

"The third martini is always a mistake."

"Then you've made a lot of mistakes in your life," she replied. "It's going to take me decades to catch up."

"You can make up ground after I'm dead, you know."

"I'll be too depressed to drink after you're dead. I'd rather drink now."

"I see your point, and it's wise. Too bad neither of us is going to remember this conversation."

Once upon a time, Sheyene Foster Lager liked a cigarette with her drink. In those days, as long as there was something in her glass, smoke should unfurl from her lips with every fourth or fifth breath. In the early stages of our relationship, she hid the fact that she smoked. When I finally caught her, squatting on a step by the front door of her apartment, listening to The Pretenders, she almost set her ass on fire as she tried to stuff the cigarette out behind her back.

"I didn't know you smoked," I said, trying not to laugh as she brushed sparks off the backside of her blue jeans.

"I don't, really," she assured me. "Only when I'm stressed."

"And how often are you stressed?"

"Not often...every once in a while."

I didn't know it yet, but not long after we got married, she would be stressed 20 to 30 times a day. For the moment, I simply asked: "Why didn't you want me to know you smoked?"

"You told me you don't like women who smoke."

"No, I said I thought smoking was unattractive."

"Well, in that case, I'm sorry I deceived you, because unattractive is exactly what I'm going for."

At first she smoked Marlboro Lights, then Camel Lights, before finally settling on American Spirit Ultra Lights. *Pure 100% American tobacco*, she'd state proudly, *just like the Native Americans invented it.*

Your patriotism is exceeded only by your restraint.

Thank you. Ready for a cigar?

When I was in my early 20's, before I'd written a word of fiction, I'd smoked a goose-neck pipe in order to look like a writer. Or an intellectual. Or something else I didn't understand. When I finally realized what a dickhead smoking a pipe made me, I switched to cigars every once in a while. Which meant about one a month, until after the first year of my first marriage, when I lost interest and stopped altogether. When Sheyene Foster Lager the Smokestack came along, I needed to do something to be sociable. So I began to allow myself one cigar a week. Then one a day. Then sometimes two or three.

You're ruining my health, I'd occasionally observe.

You can't live forever, she'd reply. *Besides, you love it. Want another martini?*

The third martini is always a mistake.

Well, nobody's perfect.

When my two younger kids, Daniel and Rachael, were over, we'd both make sure they understood that smoking was bad for you, and not to be copied. Their older brothers, David and Michael, already smoked, and frankly the shared ritual of cigarettes had made it easier for them to become friends with Sheyene. From time to time, all four of us claimed we were going to quit. David was the first to actually manage it.

When we moved to the edge of Wildcat Ridge in Manhattan, Kansas in 2000, Sheyene and I decided we would never smoke in the house. For most of the year, smoking outdoors made life more comfortable for everyone, especially our non-smoking guests. And it was pleasant to sit around the patio table with our neighbors Kari and James, all four of us sending rhythmical bursts of smoke into the Kansas sky like reports from the artillery range at

Fort Riley.

Then there was winter. Sheyene's addiction drove her outdoors, no matter what the weather, and I would sit shivering beside her, struggling to keep up my end of the conversation while my teeth clattered like piston rods in a Ford Pinto climbing a steep hill.

One bitterly cold January morning, I walked away from the computer to find Sheyene sitting in a lawn chair on the back patio, two inches of fresh snow scraped off the plastic seat. The temperature was five degrees, and the snow gleamed white off everything but her and the chair's green back and legs. Her back was to the window, and I watched her for a few moments. Her long terry cloth bathrobe, a slightly lighter shade of green than the chair, shrouded her body from neck to ankle. A gray woolen stocking cap and muffler concealed her head and neck, and her feet were covered by black leather boots. I would later discover that beneath the robe she wore thick cotton sweats and a down-filled coat. One thing I could see clearly. Between the first two fingers of one of her black leather gloves, a Camel filter-tip flickered like the promise of an early spring. Her exhalations came in two distinct forms: white rose-shaped blossoms of crystallized carbon dioxide, followed by longer steam-whistle drafts of nicotine and tar-laden carbon monoxide, which hung heavier in the still air before dissolving into the brilliant white background.

Finally, I shoved open the French doors and asked: "What are you doing out there?"

"Living," she replied.

The following spring, we moved three doors down the street to a bigger house with a better view from the ridge. From the cul de sac, the stone house at 800 Wildcat Ridge looked like a one-story rancher. But it was actually a two-story dug into a promontory on the ridge. My study was a bedroom on the upper floor, with a great view of the sloping woods along Wildcat Creek, which meandered about 200 feet below, and even a sliver of the Flint Hills on the horizon about four miles to the south. Sheyene's study was on the lower floor, a small windowless room filled from floor to ceiling with books. In that closed space with no natural light, she spent four to eight hours each day grading student essays and banging away on her MFA thesis.

The upper and lower floors of the new house were sealed off from each other by a door at each end of the connecting stairwell. When I suggested designating the lower floor as a smoking zone, Sheyene said "Are you sure?"

"Let me put it this way: We're both more likely to live through the winter."

In the evenings, after Daniel and Rachael had been safely returned to their mother at the house on 14th street, life at Steve and Sheyene Foster Lager's house inevitably sank into the gin and tobacco haze of the lower floor. Our friends Jen and Dane, both nonsmokers, would somehow bear the smoldering vapors of Sheyene's study, ventilated by only a fan and an open door. Dane likes his beer, but Jen is an epileptic and occasional sleepwalker. Red wine is particularly risky for her. In the early years of our friendship, she tried to keep up with the rest of us, until experience taught everyone Jen's proper role was ironic observer. Consequently, our conversations seldom reminded her of the sophisticated banter of 1930s movies. *Itchy and Scratchy; that's who you guys are,* Jen would tell Sheyene Foster Lager and me. And so it went, three of us drinking, four of us talking, into the early hours of the morning. When Jen and Dane were ready to leave, they would wave their arms to get our attention, like sailors signaling with semaphores on a foggy sea.

Want to make me another one, sweetie?

The third martini is always a mistake.

Yes, but who's counting?

The nights on the ridge tumbled softly by, like fog rolling into San Francisco Bay. Did Sheyene Foster Lager and I drink too much during our days on the ridge? *How can it be too much when we're still standing?* Sheyene asked one night from the floor beneath her desk.

On my 53rd birthday, Dane, a graphic artist and animator, presented me with a picture he'd created on a computer: Three martini glasses. The first glass is empty and overturned; a bare toothpick lies just beyond its rim. The second glass is also empty, but stands upright, its own exhausted toothpick resting comfortably in the glass. The third glass brims with promise, filled with what one can only hope is good gin. Two green olives with pimentos list on their toothpick against the side of the glass. In the lower part of the picture a red arrow with a #3 points toward the third glass. Below the arrow a caption reads: The Mistake Martini.

Shy and Lost Her Feller is almost totally fiction. If Sheyene ever lost a man, it would not be from shyness. "Why do you want to marry an old fart like me?" I asked her on our way to the civil ceremony in Olathe, Kansas, a decade ago.

"I've always preferred older men," she replied. "Young men are stupid and scared. They never say anything interesting. Before you, I always had to teach them everything. How to talk, how to kiss, you name it. Marriage shouldn't be that much work."

Sometimes the only possible response is laughter.

On the other hand, in certain situations, Shy and Lost Her Feller is truly shy. For example, whenever life threatens to require her to speak to someone besides me on the telephone.

Why do you want ME to call the plumber?

Because I'm not going to be here; you're the one whose schedule needs to be accommodated.

So tell him when I'll be here.

Or when a name, any name, comes up on the caller ID.

Don't answer that.

Why not?

I don't want to talk right now.

OK, but why not?

I wouldn't know what to say.

It's your grandmother, for Christsake.

I'll call her back. You know I will.

She will, of course. Today or tomorrow, whenever Shy and Lost Her Feller musters the strength to send her polite girly girl voice, the one she uses with family and strangers, chirping along the wires. Her Gal Noir voice–the quick, sarcastic, tough-as-nails bitch voice she uses with friends and enemies–requires props.

Don't answer; I'll call her back.

But it's Shelle; you love Shelle.

I do, but Shelle's going through some rough stuff—and I'm out of cigarettes. I'll call her back after I pick up a pack at Dillons.

The Kid and The Old Lady are the two public faces of Sheyene. In her mid-twenties, she was regularly mistaken for a teenager—unless she was with me. In our early days, strangers often mistook The Kid for my daughter. But no more. Somehow, in the eyes of almost everyone, she has become The Old Fart's Old Lady. *You two are soul mates,* our L.A. friends now tell us. The Old Lady thinks she knows the reason for this. I never really had a childhood, she reminds me. *When I wasn't helping Mom hold her life together, I was helping my Grandpa Poppy work in the potato patch or apply Bondo to his '48 Ford pickup. I've liked older men from the beginning.*

The Kid still asks me how to pronounce words. Recalcitrant. Mendacious. Egregious. Milieu. The Kid knows no fear: When we were first together, she would stomp the accelerator of her '87 Nissan 200 SX like a 16-year-old boy racing a rival down a back road to the lake. *Slow down or you'll kill us both,* I'd whimper. *Live hard, die young* was her reply. *Too late for me,* I pled to no avail.

The Old Lady informs me I'm still a little boy. *Don't do that—somebody might SEE you...Let's get something straight, Mister: I pay all the bills, I cook most of the meals, I do the laundry, and you can't even pick up your damn underwear...GROW UP!*

The Kid always wants to know if she has embarrassed herself in front of our friends and colleagues. *Was I OK? Did I do anything bad? I didn't say anything stupid, did I? Are you sure I was OK? I mean really...was I OK?*

The Old Lady offers timely, constructive criticism of my own behavior. *You are a fucking moron. Did you ever once stop and think about how I might feel about that? Or do you just sit around pounding your dick all day?*

The Kid takes on a new identity each month: Gal Noir, naturalist, marathon runner, memoirist, editor, baton twirler, yoga student, math tutor. Soon after we moved into our new house on the promontory, I discovered that the lower level was not merely The Kid's smoking den; it was also her dance studio. In the evening she would slap Concrete Blonde on the stereo and turn the volume up loud enough to wake the lions at Sunset Zoo. Then she would spin, sidestep, leap, and sway. I enjoyed watching her do this, and she took advantage to get whatever she wanted.

Then one afternoon I came home from campus and found her twirling round and round in a pink tutu with matching toe shoes. Her face was flushed pinker than her outfit, a shade I've seen only on the buttocks of infants with diaper rash.

"What's all this, sweetie?"

"I'm going to take ballet!"

"That's terrific...but why?"

"I took ballet when I was a kid."

"I see. And now..."

"It just makes me feel good—OK? Watch this pirouette!"

The Old Lady cannot be intimidated by the difference in our ages, or anything else. *You think just because you can swat carpenter bees out of the air with your bare hand that you're some kind of a man? That's a skill for retards, buster. How often did your momma drop you on your head when you were a baby?*

The Kid honestly believes she is stronger than a grown man. When we're traveling and I insist on lugging the heaviest bags, she complains I'm trying to make her look like a girl. When I slipped on a patch of ice in the driveway and broke my ankle attempting to save a bottle of scotch, she wanted to carry me to the car on her back. "I can do it," she insisted, getting down on her hands and knees in the snow. "Just crawl up on my back and hold on. I'll carry you piggy-back."

"No thanks, Tarzan. It's probably just a sprain."

When I attempted to put weight on my left foot and the truth did not set me free, we compromised.

"OK, I'll lean on your shoulder if you promise to take it slow."

"Whatever you say, Jane. At least you saved the scotch."

The Old Lady is our financial advisor and investment banker. *Don't throw away that plastic bag! We can use it to wrap sandwiches...We should really get the 8200 instead. It's got the better screen and faster processor. You can burn CDs and DVDs on it—think of the money we'll save...Why do I want to go to Toys R Us in February? Everything's half-price now; that's why. We'll get our Christmas shopping done ten months early...Don't use the gold credit card; use the blue one. The blue one's 0% interest on new purchases.*

The Kid is a techno whiz. Although my father was an electrician and I was using a computer when she thought a brassier was something you strapped on a horse, The Kid sees no point in my messing with anything involving electronics. *Look, I can either install the program for you, or I can explain how to install it. The former will take three clicks; the latter will take about as long as it took to impeach Bill Clinton.* Despite her caustic wit, explanations are not The Kid's strong suit. The Kid knows how, but not why. Her relationship with technology is the product of trial and error, expressed by muscle memory.

Wait a minute: How did you do that?

Easy. You just click here and pull this down, then click here.

But how did you know to click there?

Oh, you just keep clicking until you get what you want.

But you clicked only three times.

So? Why waste energy?

The Old Lady is an efficiency expert and control freak, the Martha Stewart of the Heller house. The Old Lady knows both how and why. *Don't fold your socks into a ball like that; just stuff one ankle into the other like this, and leave the foot parts hanging out. That way you can see if the toes match ...No, no, no. Never put the clothes in before the detergent. First, you pour the detergent into the machine, then close the lid and run some water for about five seconds. THEN you put the clothes in. That way you dilute the detergent, and it doesn't leave stains...No, no, no. If you do it that way, it'll just...never mind, I'll do it.*

Since she turned my life upside-down, Sheyene's hair has faded from strawberry red to the color of ripe wheat. But Woody Woodpecker and

One Non-Blonde have little to do with hair color. They are polar opposites, the daily manifestations of Sheyene's inexorable mood swings. Woody Woodpecker is bubbly and upbeat, a child of mischievous joy. Woody dances around me like a pixie, bounds into my arms like a Labrador retriever, knocks me flat with her exuberance, swallows me whole with her love. *I LOVE our life...I love YOU, you silly old fart.* Woody tackles me in the kitchen and drags me to the bedroom. She grabs me by the ears and pulls me inside her. I swim dizzy in a sea of love, never come up for air. *Are you happy with me?* she whispers. *I'm happy with you.* Woody makes plans, dreams dreams, maps out our future. *I'm going to retire you to island of Lana`i. I'll teach my online classes, and you'll write. We'll have a big dog and a small child.*

Then, at the sound of a single syllable sung in a minor key, or for no reason whatsoever, Woody vanishes. Like the apparitions who accost me in the solitude of my own dreams, she is simply gone. But unlike the troubled woman played by Joann Woodward in *Three Faces of Eve*, or the ghosts who walk with me every day, I cannot call her back, cannot conjure her up at will. Woody loves me, but exists apart from me, and her joy is fleeting. I can fuel her passion, nurture her joy, but I cannot sustain it. At some point she will dance too close to the flame that burns somewhere just outside her soul, and poof: One Non-Blonde.

One Non-Blonde is bitter and recriminating. *I hate our life. HATE it. I try to be upbeat, I try to be happy, I try to give you everything you want—and you respond with THIS.* One Non-Blonde cannot be deterred, cannot be banished. One Non-Blonde is here until she feels like leaving. *Oh no, THIS is what you get, THIS is what you prefer, THIS is what you wanted. Now you've got it.* One Non-Blonde is unsentimental. *Oh, and I'm supposed to think everything's better now because of a hug? Well, think again, Mister.* One Non-Blonde broods, feeds her anger. She turns away, shuts me out. One Non-Blonde slaps on headphones and cranks the stereo up full-volume. Roaring inside her skull, wounded women sing the blues. Seven Year Bitch, Alanis Morrisette, Four Non-Blondes, Violent Fems, The Pretenders, Edda James, Concrete Blonde. These are One Non-Blonde's gals, including the men. One Non-Blonde rocks and sways and mouths the words of her private siren songs, while I creep around the edges of the music in a ghostly silence.

I cannot change her mood, for One Non-Blonde is unforgiving. She sees no point in trying any more. *I've heard this before. Nothing changes.* She packs her bags in the middle of the night, storms out of the house in a freezing rain with no coat, without her glasses or contacts, disappears down the ridge, into the woods, into thin air. One Non-Blonde leaves me gutted, a disemboweled fish flopping on the floor. Leaves me numb and quivering in her wake. Leaves me with nothing. Leaves me.

Then somehow, from the opposite sides of the ridge, we crawl back to each other.

I'm sorry.

I'm sorry too.

Sometime later, when she's strong again, I see the Sheyene I love most.

Cayenne Pepper is spicy hot. She improves my taste, and makes life taste better. She is all the other Sheyenes packed into one radioactive seed. She is fire and ice, yin and yang, youth and age, wit and wisdom. She hurts and soothes, burns and burns hotter. She is best in measured doses, for a little of her goes all the way to your soul. But there are no recipes for Cayenne Pepper, and no small portions. She seasons each day like a driving rain. She erupts with Pele's fire, chills with an arctic gale. She overwhelms my senses, picks apart my mind. She loves, hates, dreams faster than the speed of darkness; I shudder in the sonic booms of her voice and touch. *You must learn how to stay more even*, I advise her. But this is not possible. Cayenne Pepper burns with an inextinguishable salty sweetness that sears my arteries, explodes my heart. *I want to be around you all the time*, she tells me. *We don't need any friends.* But she doesn't mean this. Cayenne Pepper needs, wants, and fears like anyone else, but accepts no help. I watch powerless as the events of each day mortar and pestle her into a fine powder. Then, miraculously, at some point that same day or the next, she re-sprouts, bursting into bloom like a flaming rose. At her core, Cayenne Pepper is resilient, indomitable. *I can do this,* she tells me again and again. *We can do this.*

Yes, I always reply. *Yes, we can.*

A few months after we moved into our new house on Wildcat Ridge, we hosted an informal writing workshop for graduate students, alumni, and a few other folks from the community. Jen and Dane were there, of course, and our still-close neighbors Kari and James. Sheyene's former classmate Marissa was in town from Detroit, along with maybe a dozen friends who had come to share poems and stories, along with good food and conversation. Sheyene was in hostess mode, filling glasses and charming everyone with her insults while I finished up the lamb curry, peppers with cauliflower, and cucumber raita. As we set up the buffet, I wondered: Which Sheyene will we see tonight?

It didn't take long to find out. Shortly after dinner, in the middle of the workshop, through the living room picture window I noticed Sheyene searching the short backyard above the ridge with a flashlight. I excused myself and slipped out the back door.

"Jen's disappeared," Sheyene said. She had some merlot before she came over."

I shook my head in the darkness. "The first bottle of red wine is always a mistake."

"I had her lay down in our bed a few minutes ago. Now she's nowhere in the house. The kitchen door was open. Dane and I think she's sleepwalking."

"Jesus. On the ridge?" In places, the curling slope below us was almost vertical, with drops of ten feet and more.

"Dane's already half way down, looking."

A few minutes later, Kari and James had provided extra flashlights, and everyone was searching.

Sheyene organized the searchers, spreading them out to cover as much territory as possible. "Shouldn't we call 911?" someone asked.

"Not now," Sheyene said. "Not unless we can't find her. Jen wouldn't want that."

Moments later, beams swept the dark ridge as if a killer were on the loose. Fearing Jen might have walked off in the opposite direction, through the neighborhood, I jumped into our Stratus and drove all the nearby streets, looking for Jen's shadow in the shadows.

After 20 minutes, I gave up. It was time to call 911.

In our Kansas days Sheyene and I had no cell phones, so I had to return to the house on the ridge. When I neared the cul de sac, I spotted the one thing I did not want to see: an ambulance.

Kari met me at the front door. "She's OK," she said, grabbing my elbow. "She's down in the den. The paramedics are checking her over."

"Thank god …Who found her?"

"Sheyene and James. Jen was pretty far down the slope. She'd wrapped herself up in a blanket, and it got tangled in the brush just before the really steep part. Apparently, she just lay down right there and went to sleep."

We were heading down the stairs and into the lower level now, past a line of relieved faces. "Why is the door to the den closed?"

Kari brought me to a halt. "James said Jen was still pretty much asleep when he and Dane started carrying her up the hill. Then about halfway up, she started going into convulsions. They weren't violent, but they went on for a while. Dane said not to worry, and they carried her on up. Sheyene told us not to call an ambulance because it would upset Jen if she woke up and found herself surrounded by paramedics. Apparently somebody called anyway. Turned out Sheyene was right. When Jen woke up, she told everyone she definitely didn't want to see any medics. But by then they were already on their way. Sheyene didn't want to let them in, but once they've been called, you have to admit them. When Jen saw them, she started to freak. Dane and Sheyene calmed her down. I think she's OK now."

"So why's the door closed?"

"Sheyene closed it. She got angry when the paramedics arrived. Then she said there were too many people hanging around, and Jen needed some room to breathe and recover."

"She's probably right," I replied.

"Yeah, well, I wouldn't go in there, if I were you."

"Don't worry," I said, pushing the door open. "I'm family."

Inside, I found Jen lying on the small black sofa. A male and female paramedic hovered nearby, watching her closely. Dane and Sheyene were even closer to Jen. Dane sat on the sofa arm beside her Jen's head, squeezing her right hand, a look of unmitigated relief on his face. Sheyene knelt at Jen's feet, holding her other hand.

"It doesn't matter, dearie," Sheyene cooed. "They just want to make sure you're all right."

"Well, I don't know why I can't just go home. I feel fine now. Why can't I just go home?"

"You do appear to be stable now," the female paramedic conceded. "But to be safe, I think we should take you to Mercy and let a doctor have a look at you."

Jen shook her head. "Nope. No way." Then, in a softer voice, "Really, I'm all right now."

"She is," Dane assured the paramedic. "We've been here before."

"I understand," the paramedic said. "But just to be safe..."

They talked about it for a few more minutes, but it was already clear Jen was not going to get into the ambulance. Eventually my gaze turned to Sheyene. She was letting the paramedics do their job, but through it all she continued to kneel beside Jen like a vigilant guard dog. Her face, though, was clear and radiant as a full moon. She watched Jen's face. If the slightest bit of doubt or fear or anger appeared, Sheyene squeezed her hand.

"I'll be back in a minute," I said, and slide the door open again.

Everyone was waiting upstairs.

"Jen's going to be fine. She's going to hang around here for a while, then go home. Thanks for all your help, everyone. You were great. We appreciate it more than I can say."

"Sheyene got really pissed at us," one of my students said.

"Then you're lucky to be standing upright, my good man. Thanks again, everyone. I'm sure Jen will communicate with us all in a few days. Until then, take care of yourselves. Drive carefully."

After Jen signed a release and the paramedics finally left, Jen and Dane and Sheyene and I remained in the den for about an hour. I watched our friends slowly decompress, easing themselves back into the world. We joked a little, cried a little, relearning how to breathe. Sheyene sat or knelt beside

Jen practically the entire time. But not too close. No one would suffocate on the ridge that night.

"I'm sorry," Jen said for the hundredth time when we finally walked them to their car.

"You have nothing to be sorry for, dearie," Sheyene assured her for the hundredth time. "Get some sleep and lay off the red wine."

"Thanks for everything, guys," Dane said.

As we watched them drive off, Sheyene said, "I'm going to find out who called 911 and twist his balls off."

"Sweetie, whoever called was just trying to help."

"I don't care. When I get hold of him, his ass is lemon grass."

I looked at her for a moment. "Cayenne Pepper."

She turned to me. "What?"

"That's who you are tonight."

She rolled her eyes and leaned against my shoulder.

"And you are just plain silly...I'm exhausted. Let's go to bed."

Nearly eight years have now passed since Jen walked halfway down the slope of Wildcat Ridge in her sleep. She and Dane live in Virginia. Sheyene and I have moved on to L.A., where I direct a creative writing program and she teaches English courses online. Instead of paying modest rent for a five-bedroom house on a ridge, we pay three to four times as much for a two-bedroom apartment. Sheyene is in her early thirties now, and I have shuddered past sixty. But the age difference is hardly our biggest challenge. The biggest challenge is Truman Francis Heller, age three at this writing. Truman favors Sheyene, thank god. Same puckish blue eyes and rascally grin, same amber wheat hair as his mother's current shade. Charming, impish, naughty when he can get away with it, Truman wears an early Beatles end-curled mop top to cover his sticky-outie elfin ears, but otherwise looks like he's going to trouble the girls no end. *I see a bird, I smell a house*, he says, gazing off the balcony of our 7th floor apartment. His mother melts at such phrasings; his older brothers and sister laugh on the phone from somewhere on the island of O`ahu, where they all now live. We'll probably wind up calling him True, but at this age only one nickname captures him: Cayenne Toddler.

Most would say that motherhood has transformed Sheyene. To an extent, they're right. Gone, for example, is The Kid who takes risks with her own life and the lives of others. *I want plug protectors for EVERY outlet Truman can reach...You're going 40 in a 35 zone, damn it—SLOW DOWN!*

But the undeniable truth is that somewhere beneath her not-quite-as-smooth skin and our new West Coast circumstances, all the Sheyenes I can't resist are still there, combined into a more seasoned, still super spicy form: Cayenne Mother.

You're the biggest baby in this house, Cayenne Mother likes to remind me. Nevertheless, I have to stand in line for her attention, behind Truman and the dog (Dachshund Hammett, aka "Dash"). *I wanted a small child and a BIG dog*, the Woody Woodpecker in Cayenne Mother says, *but little dogs are fun too*. Despite three devoted men in her life, things could be better for Cayenne Mother. After a dozen failed attempts, which by only the slimmest of margins produced no fatalities, in 2006 Sheyene gave up cigarettes. My cigars disappeared in dutiful support. We hoped these sacrifices would lead to greater health and longevity. But for the last several years Sheyene has suffered from a mysterious, debilitating, so-far-impossible-to-diagnose form of rheumatoid arthritis. Or Lupus. Or Lyme Disease. Or something else. On some days the affliction is so painful she cannot lift her left arm above her shoulder. Nights are worse, and I occasionally wake to the sound of her whimpering. For the most part, though, she bears her malady with the stoicism of one so accustomed to pain that the last time she had a tooth filled, the dentist used no anesthesia. The latest drug prescribed for her mystery condition would require her to give up drinking. No way! Sheyene Foster Lager cries out. The Kid and The Old Lady team up to research non-traditional methods of treatment. *A vegan diet*, The Kid suggests. *A bottle of scotch and something hard to bite down on*, counters The Old Lady.

All the Sheyenes associate most of our problems with Los Angeles. On their worst days, One Non-Blonde speaks the loudest: *I hate L.A. I want grass, trees with leaves that fall off. I want not outrageously expensive. I want to go an entire week without seeing anyone who's criminally insane. I want to live somewhere where Truman can play outdoors and I won't freak. I want...anywhere but here.*

And yet, through all of it, Cayenne Mother somehow abides. Youth and age, fire and ice, tenderness and rage. Despite her life partner's insensitivity, stupidity, and increasing resemblance to a moldy cigar store Indian with no cigar, Cayenne Mother persists. As the years pass, I wonder, with increasing urgency, what I can do to help give her the strength necessary to face whatever lies ahead.

Some nights, when the future is too troubling, I lie awake and think about the night in Kansas when Jen went sleepwalking on the slope of the Wildcat Ridge. Long after the ambulance, Jen and Dane, and all the other guests had departed, Sheyene and I lay in bed, staring into each other's eyes in exhausted relief. When at last her eyes closed, through the bedroom window I watched the sliver of a moon slip behind a cloud, and I began to dream.

Sheyene and I are standing on the edge of an abyss. Beneath and beyond us, all I can see are white, white clouds beneath a crystal blue sky. I don't know why we are here, nor what we are supposed to do next. Nevertheless, I hear Sheyene say:

I can do this. We can do this.

Yes, I want to reply. *Yes, we can.*

But this time my answer is different.

I rip open my shirt, sending buttons flying. With the fingernails of my right hand, I begin to claw at my exposed chest. I do not bleed, not a single drop, as I methodically strip away layers of skin, then dig down through taut muscle, right on through slick white bone, until at last I can see quivering black nerves around the throbbing red apple of my heart. With my free hand, I take one of Sheyene's.

Here, I say. *Touch me right here.*

About the Editors

Walter Cummins's fourth short story collection, *The End of the Circle*, was published in 2010. His stories, essays, and reviews have appeared in many magazines. Co-founder of Serving House Books, he is Editor Emeritus of *The Literary Review* and a faculty member in the Fairleigh Dickinson University's low-residency MFA in Creative Writing Program and the MA in Creative Writing and Literature for Educators. His website is www.waltercummins. com

Thomas E. Kennedy's latest novels are appearing from Bloomsbury—*In the Company of Angels (2010)* and *Falling Sideways* (2011) to be followed soon after with the remaining two novels of the *Copenhagen Quartet*. Recent essays appear in *New Letters*, *Epoch*, *Ecotone*, and *ServingHouseJournal*. With Walter Cummins, he is co-founder of Serving House Books and teaches at the Fairleigh Dickinson University low-residency MFA in Creative Writing Program. His website is www.thomasekennedy.com

About the Authors and Translators

Martin Aitken gave up university tenure to translate literature and listen to The Fall. His translations of Danish literature have appeared both in book form and in numerous journals and periodicals including *FENCE*, *Calque*, *AGNI*, *The Literary Review*, *PRISM International*, and *The Boston Review*.

Renée Ashley's most recent book is *Basic Heart*, winner of the X. J. Kennedy Poetry Prize. She is on the faculty of Fairleigh Dickinson University's low-residency MFA in Creative Writing and the MA in Creative Writing and Literature for Educators. A portion of her poem "First Book of the Moon" is etched in marble in Penn Station Terminal in Manhattan, part of a permanent installation by the artist Larry Kirkland.

Duff Brenna is the author of six novels. He is the recipient of an AWP Award for Best Novel, a National Endowment for the Arts Award, a *South Florida Sun-Sentinel* Award for Favorite Book of the year, a *Milwaukee Magazine* Best Short Story of the Year Award, and a Pushcart Honorable Mention. His work has been translated into six languages. His website is www.duffbrenna.com

Tom Dunne is the author of many works, most recently *The Big Book of Danish Caramels*.

Niels Hav is a full time poet and short story writer with prestigious awards from The Danish Arts Council. In English he has *We Are Here*, published by Book Thug, and poetry and fiction in numerous magazines including *The*

Literary Review, Shearsman, Exile, The Los Angeles Review, and *PRISM International.*

Steve Heller directs the MFA in Creative Writing Program at Antioch University Los Angeles. His latest book is a collection of nonfiction, *What We Choose to Remember,* from Serving House Books. New work forthcoming in *Flint Hills Review* and other journals. He is working on a new novel and a collection of new and selected stories of Hawaii.

H. L. Hix teaches in the creative writing MFA at the University of Wyoming. His most recent book, *First Fire, Then Birds: Obsessionals 1985-2010,* was published in September 2010 by Etruscan Press. His website is www.hlhix.com.

Steve Kowit insists that although people often assume poets do not earn much money, he and the Romance novelist Nora Roberts have a combined annual income of sixty million dollars. He earns the rest of his income as a male stripper at Chippendale's.

Line-Maria Lång is half Swedish, half Danish, and lives in Copenhagen. Her debut collection, *Rat King (Rottekonge),* appeared in 2009 from the Danish house, Rosinante. Other translations from that book will appear soon in *Southern Review* and elsewhere.

Alexandra Marshall is the author of five novels: *The Court of Common Pleas, Something Borrowed, The Brass Bed, Tender Offer,* and *Gus in Bronze.* She has also published a work of nonfiction, *Still Waters,* to accompany the PBS "Nova" film of the same title. She has been a Guest Columnist for *The Boston Globe* and a film critic for *The American Prospect,* and her essays, feature stories, and opinion pieces have appeared in a variety of journals. Her short stories have been published in *Ploughshares, Agni, Five Points, The Cape Cod Voice,* and *Hunger Mountain.* A piece called "Sukiyaki Song" was included in the recent Serving House Books anthology, *The Book of Worst Meals.*

Laura McCullough is the author of *Panic,* winner of a Kinereth Genseler Award from Alice James Books, *Speech Acts*, *What Men Want, and The Dancing Bear*, as well the chapbooks, *Women and Other Hostages* and *Elephant Anger*. She has served as poetry editor of *Serving House Journal*.

Dorthe Nors is one of Denmark's foremost new writers. She is the author of three novels as well as the highly acclaimed collection of stories *Kantslag* [Karate Chop]. Her latest book *Dage* [Days] was recently published by Samleren of Copenhagen. Some of her recent stories have appeared in English in *AGNI*, *The Boston Review*, *FENCE*, and *New Letters*.

Lance Olsen is author of more than 20 books of and about innovative fiction, including, most recently, *Calendar of Regrets* (FC2, 2010). He teaches experimental narrative theory and practice at the University of Utah and serves as fiction editor of *Western Humanities Review*.

Pamela Painter's new collection of stories, *Wouldn't You Like to Know*, was published in 2010. She has written two previous story collections, *Getting to Know the Weather* and *The Long and Short of It*, and is co-author of the textbook *What If?* Her stories appear in numerous journals and anthologies, and have won three Pushcart Prizes and AGNI's John Cheever Award for Fiction. Painter teaches at Emerson College in Boston.

David R. Poe lives in Paris with his wife and son. His stories have appeared in *Prairie Schooner*, *Cimarron Review*, *The Literary Review*, and *Story Quarterly* as well as in Australian and French journals.

Ladette Randolph is the author of the award-winning short story collection *This Is Not the Tropics*, and the author of the novel, *A Sandhills Ballad*, which was a 2009 *New York Times* Editor's Choice, and a finalist for both ForeWord book of the year and the WILLA Award. She is editor-in-chief of *Ploughshares* magazine and on the faculty of Emerson College's Writing, Literature, and Publishing department.

Robert Stewart edits *New Letters* magazine and is author of *Outside Language: Essays* (Helicon Nine Editions, a finalist in the PEN Center USA Literary Awards for 2004; and winner of the Thorpe Menn Award), *Plumbers* (poems, BkMk Press), and others.

Susan Tekulve is the author of three short story collections, *Savage Pilgrims*, *Wash Day*, and *My Mother's War Stories*. Her short fiction and essays have appeared in *Shenandoah*, *New Letters*, *Best New Writing 2007*, *The Indiana Review*, *Denver Quarterly*, *Puerto del Sol*, *Prairie Schooner*, *Beloit Fiction Journal*, *Crab Orchard Review*, and *Black Warrior Review*. She has been awarded scholarships from the Sewanee Writers' Conference and the Bread Loaf Writers' Conference.

www.ingramcontent.com/pod-product-compliance
Lightning Source LLC
Chambersburg PA
CBHW031838170626
46807CB00004B/1520